# Crash Course in Public Library Administration

# Crash Course in Public Library Administration

**Wayne Disher**

**Crash Course**

AN IMPRINT OF ABC-CLIO, LLC
Santa Barbara, California • Denver, Colorado • Oxford, England

**Library of Congress Cataloging-in-Publication Data**

Disher, Wayne.
   Crash course in public library administration / Wayne Disher.
       p. cm. — (Crash course series)
   Includes bibliographical references and index.
   ISBN 978-1-59884-465-8 (pbk. : acid-free paper) 1. Public libraries—
United States—Administration. I. Title.
Z678.6.D47 2010
025.1'974—dc22            2010028474

ISBN: 978-1-59884-465-8

14 13 12 11 10   1 2 3 4 5

This book is also available on the World Wide Web as an eBook.
Visit www.abc-clio.com for details.

Libraries Unlimited
An Imprint of ABC-CLIO, LLC

ABC-CLIO, LLC
130 Cremona Drive, P.O. Box 1911
Santa Barbara, California 93116-1911

This book is printed on acid-free paper ∞
Manufactured in the United States of America

# Contents

# Preface

This book is intended to present a quick and informative look at public administration principles and how they are often applied in public institutions, particularly the public library environment. Rather than attempting to be a "how to" manual or a detailed textbook, this book is intended to provide brief snapshots of the topic at hand. The reader will find general and basic guidelines, fundamentals, and rationale that will help library professionals who are less familiar with the field of public administration find logical answers to administrative questions beyond the standard, "because that's the way it has to be done." Perhaps the reader needs to refresh skills he or she once knew, or perhaps the interested student wants a stepping stone of sorts to begin learning more on the topic. Whatever the reason, it is assumed that students will enhance the knowledge obtained through this book with supplemental material on specific topics of interest or need.

# Introduction

John Donne, the noted seventeenth-century English poet, famously wrote that "No man is an island, entire of itself." The same must also be said of a public library. Public libraries do not stand entire of themselves, devoid of governance from a parent body. Every public library exists within a government framework down through which funding, policy, and control flows. The study of this process flow may be familiar to some who took political science courses in school. It involves many relevant theories and concepts useful to the public library manager: economic, social, management, and administrative law; political science; budgeting; and rules of order. When applying these concepts to public institutions and public policy, this field of study is known as *public administration.* Public administration focuses on the means by which much of the political, economic, social and legal theory can enhance our democratic values of equality, justice, and the "public good." Public library administration is no different. It uses the same principles but applies them to enhancing public library service for the public good.

Looking at your own community governing structure, you would likely find more than a few—and quite likely a great many!—officials, politicians, and managers who have earned postgraduate degrees in the field of public administration. This has made them quite skillful in the use of public administration practices to create laws, ordinances, and services that benefit the public good. Public libraries depend so heavily on the support of the governing body to which they belong that it often surprises many to learn that public administration is rarely—if ever—a part of postgraduate-level library science studies.

When I first became a library director, my lack of understanding of public administrative principles temporarily hampered my ability to plan services easily and effectively and to understand how to guide my library efficiently through the political process to achieve specific goals. "Does my city council need to approve accepting a state or federal grant?" "How does the library board function in the city structure?" "When do I start planning my department budget?" "Why is there such a potential for conflict between the library commission and the city council?" and "Why can't I just call each of the library board members individually and ask them for approval to set a policy?" These were just a few of the many questions I had that could easily have been answered with a proper understanding of public administration. With this in mind, readers should heed the warning that "no man is an island" and learn to navigate the political landscape that is public library administration.

# CHAPTER 1

## Local Government and Its Services

### What Is a Public Library?

Defining a public library isn't a difficult task. In fact, the definition is usually provided for us because public libraries are normally established and defined as part of a state law or education code. These regulations help us with our definition and provide certain criteria that government entities must follow to create a public library. These criteria include things such as the following: the public library must exist to serve a specified community or region; the library must provide some sort of organized collection of materials, staff, and a building; and the library must provide a schedule during which the public may access all of the above. All of this must be supported in some way with public funds. These funds generally come from revenue obtained through a city's collection of taxes, fees, other charges, or a combination of these.

The 2009 American Library Association fact sheet reports that there are slightly more than 122,350 libraries of various types in the United States. Most of these exist within public schools; however, public libraries rank as the second largest constituency in this grouping. Of the public libraries, more than two-thirds are *city* public libraries. The reader should also be aware, though, that academic, school, and special or private libraries (such as a law or medical library) also exist. The differences between these libraries refer to the institutional mission to which each library prescribes.

But what of the varying types of *public* libraries? Public libraries are provided by a city, state, county, and special districts. Because there are more *city* libraries than any other form of public library, this book will continually refer to the public library existing within a *city* government structure. This is not to say, however, that the city library is the sole form of public library available in the United States. You may well be working in one of the many county, state, or special district public libraries in American communities. The mission of the varying types of public libraries determines how each differs from the other. Essentially, however, the main difference between public libraries comes down to how, and from where, each receives its funding to operate. If it receives funding solely from the town or city, it's referred to as a "city library." If funding for library operations comes from the county's general fund, it's referred to as a "county library."

Some public libraries exist within a "special district." Special district libraries are funded through a more complicated scheme. They are normally funded by contributions from the several local governments benefiting from the services provided and who form an autonomous board authorized by legislation to tax, issue bonds, or set fees on behalf of the district.

In principle, all public libraries, regardless of their funding, are administered in the same manner. Therefore, readers can be comfortable knowing that no matter which type of public library they are interested in, the public administration lessons learned within this book can be easily applied.

# The Roots of Local Public Library Service in Local Government

The U.S. constitution allocates a significant amount of ultimate power to the federal government—for example, the power to declare war. However, it also gives practically all other powers to the individual states except those that could, conceivably, work against the good of the entire union. In laying the groundwork for this federalist government, the constitution also preserved the various forms of local government and the departments within that government that existed at that time. In the early stages of our nation's formative years, municipalities struggled with major growing pains and urgent infrastructure issues. Many state governments were seen as ineffective in dealing with such "localized" problems. As a result, the state's powers declined, and legislation duties seemed to be abdicated to the smaller municipal governments. It was at this time that local and county government became the primary point of administration.

According to the National Association of Counties (www.naco.org), there are currently about 3,100 counties in the United States, most of them suburban or rural. With only a rare exception, there is no part of a state in the United States that is not also part of a county. Owing to the state's French influence, Louisiana calls its counties "parishes"; Alaska calls its counties "boroughs." Nonetheless, they are, for all intents and purposes, the same thing. In fact, counties in the United States are still the basic political category in many of our nation's rural areas.

As urban areas grew in this country, city administrators looked for autonomy and independence from the county government restrictions. They looked at many of their urban problems as unique and often could not find support from county officials to assist in solving them. As a result, many cities incorporated, forming their own government structure to make their own decisions and spend funds as they deemed appropriate. As a result, contemporary study of government shows that most local power is now held by cities and municipalities.

The relationship between federal, state, and local governments is far more complex than one might think. Local governments, whether they be counties or cities, share a delicate tension between the need for a bit of independence to fulfill their functions and their need for the resources (particularly money) from the higher and broader levels of government to be able to do just that.

## Local Government Structure

Before turning to the administration of a public library, it will be useful to dissect the administration of the local government in which a public library exists. By doing so, the reader begins to understand operational and interdepartmental relationships. An understanding emerges of the how, why, and the way in which decisions are made in local government. Perhaps even more important, an understanding emerges of the lines of authority and the potential for library administrators to capitalize on all this information to marshal resources, plan, and budget more successfully and efficiently.

The United States Census Web site (www.census.gov) reports that two-thirds of our nation's population lives in the top 100 metropolitan areas, and more than 80 percent of Americans live in large metropolitan cities. We are no longer a rural nation. People's needs and demands from local government, from police to fire, transportation to education, and housing to library are addressed most directly by city governments. There are, broadly speaking, two major forms of local government: the council-manager form and the mayor-council form.

## The Council-Manager Form of Government

The council-manager form of government combines leadership of the municipalities' elected officials (in the form of a council or other governing body), with the necessary operational and managerial experience of a local government manager appointed by the elected body. In this form of local government, most of the municipalities' governing power is concentrated in the elected council members who have the authority to hire a city manager of their choosing to oversee the day-to-day delivery of public services.

The council-manager form of government has many benefits and strengths. For example, all council members share rights, obligations, and opportunities equally because this power is given to the council as a whole. City managers work at the will of the council as a whole and must be responsive in providing day-to-day public services to citizens; if they fail to do so, they can be replaced. Because day-to-day operations are handled by these managers, the council's members can conceivably concentrate on broader issues such as city policy and planning. Just under half of our nation's municipalities utilize the council-manager form of government.

## The Mayor-Council Form of Government

Slightly more than half of U.S. cities use the mayor-council government system. Under this form, the mayor is a position elected by the constituents and is given almost total administrative authority, as well as a clear, wide range of political independence. The mayor is given significantly more power than the other officials elected to govern. For example, mayors have the power to appoint and remove most department heads. In addition, they will prepare the budget for the council's *consideration*, but ultimately (with an effective veto power) it is the mayor's decision on how to allocate the city's funds.

In many municipalities utilizing the mayor-council form of government, the mayor is often assisted by a chief administrator who is hired and may be removed at the sole discretion of the mayor. Mayors often delegate many of their duties to the chief administrative officer or city manager; such duties include supervision of the department heads, preparation of the budget, and interdepartment coordination. However, a strong mayor who holds the power to hire and fire this manager obviously wields a great deal of influence in these operations.

## Elected Officials

In the United States, the election of local government officials looks a good deal like state and federal elections. The elected officials in a local government serve a specified term (typically two to four years). They are elected to serve the interests of the people they serve, and they are ultimately held accountable to them. However, one could argue that local-level officials enact laws and legislation that have a more direct impact on local issues than their higher-level counterparts. For example, local government decisions can determine the sort of signs that can be posted in a business and where these signs can be displayed; where cars and RVs can park; and what time underage children have to be off the streets at night. Most elected officials also have the ability to affect the library building (if not directly what happens within the facility) as well as its budget and operations.

Many local officials are civic leaders with strong ties to the community. Some may be local business owners, some may be church leaders, and some may be members of a prominent family in the community. Library administrators who pay attention to the community affiliations of the city's elected officials will sometimes find it beneficial in helping to avoid later pitfalls or open up potential avenues of support.

## The Civic Family

Before understanding the design of our library organizations, we must remember that we are not islands; we have a civic family to which we belong. At this time, it would be beneficial to obtain a copy of your civic organization chart. What does your civic organization look like? The most common civic organization is structured in a classical hierarchy of levels representing positions and departments, each tasked with jobs and responsibilities related in some way to public services. We will delve more closely into organization charts later in this book, but for now, notice who is at the top of the organization's chart and who's at the bottom? What are the relations between the organization's departments? Who reports to whom? Does this structure make sense? Why is this organization structured the way it is? These are only a few of the questions confronting students of public administration. They can be answered by understanding the principles of organization design and structure, a topic we return to in a later chapter.

# CHAPTER 2

## Public Administrators

Most of us think of public administrators as department heads, such as the library director. This is certainly true. In larger cities, however, other members of the department team can be classified as administrators. Public administrators are basically people who manage or supervise the provision of a public service. They collect and analyze statistics, help develop policy, create and track budgets, and generally ensure that government activities are provided efficiently.

If one thinks of a typical organization chart, set up in the shape of a pyramid, a city or town manager (who reports directly to the elected officials) sits at the top of the structure with individuals such as the police chief, planning director, and library director each heading up individual departments. Many managers within civic organizations are so concentrated on their own department that they often don't understand the nature of the jobs of their colleagues within the rest of the town's organization. Ignorance of the services provided by other departments and how they contribute to the public good all public administrators strive for hurts the entire organization and ultimately hurts our own department. For this reason, we will take a look at a typical civic organization's primary executives and the departments they represent. Obviously, you may not find all of the departments mentioned here in every city jurisdiction. Some may have duties combined into other departments, and some may be structured differently, utilizing other directors to oversee operations. In addition, some larger cities will have department heads not discussed here, such as parks and recreation director or director of redevelopment.

# City Manager

The city's or town's manager is the top executive in the jurisdiction. As already pointed out, depending on the form of government operating in the jurisdiction, the city manager is held accountable to the council as a whole or works specifically with the city's mayor. Managers oversee all areas of the entire organization's operations. The manager sees that services offered by each department are those that the community wants and needs. The manager selects department heads, often evaluates their performance, works with them to resolve problems, and helps them develop policy. The manager orchestrates the city's operations by crafting the operating and capital budgets, setting agendas, and serving as the appointing authority for much of the organization's personnel. The city manager spends a great deal of time acting as a liaison among elected officials, developers, department heads, community groups, and the media to ensure the city's mission, goals, and objectives are at least heard if not always met.

Because it is nearly impossible for one person to manage all aspects of the jurisdiction's operations effectively, the city manager will often delegate certain responsibilities such as department head supervision to assistant or deputy managers. However, the manager ultimately remains accountable to the elected officials and to the community to ensure that the city operates effectively and efficiently.

These persons all serve the city, and their departments maintain services for the welfare of the citizens.

## Public Safety

Perhaps the primary concern of every city, county, or other jurisdiction is public safety. How to prevent crime, protect citizens, and ensure a safe environment occupies a great deal of any jurisdiction's time and budget. It is not uncommon, in fact, for nearly 70 to 80 percent or more of a jurisdiction's operating budget to be allocated entirely toward public safety departments. The major departments operating under the public safety banner are police, fire, and, to a lesser extent, code enforcement. Because of the high-profile nature of public safety services, the executives charged with running these departments are often called upon by reporters in the local press for comments, interviews, and public statements. Because of this, the jurisdiction's manager will work closely to coordinate comments and ensure that a single, unified voice representing the organization is presented at all times.

## The Police and Fire Chiefs

Both the police chief and the fire chief serve as heads of the two largest public safety departments of a city or municipality. They are ultimately responsible to the city manager, the elected officials, and the citizens for delivering a wide range of police and fire services to their community. The chiefs determine the strategic missions of their departments, each securing necessary resources to coordinate their respective department assets. They make the final decisions on the expenditure of budgetary resources and alignment of personnel. The chiefs often work with a public community group of commissioners to develop public safety policies and provide direction to department staff in implementing them. The chiefs, particularly the police chief, must stay abreast of law changes, court decisions, and evolving regulations that may affect public safety services.

The services offered by the police and fire departments are well known to most of us. They include typical activities such as crime scene investigation, traffic control, neighborhood patrol, firefighting, fire prevention, rescue, and dispatch. Each department also is charged with at least a few atypical activities. Police departments coordinate gang suppression units, youth sports leagues, bicycle licensing, and stolen property. The fire chief is the executive responsible for inspecting places of business for fire hazards and ensuring compliance with fire regulations. The fire chief is one of the few department heads who sign off on certain development projects as cities work to approve and issue occupancy permits and related licenses. Some fire crews are often responsible for emergency response and paramedic services. The fire chief and staff investigate causes of fires and maintain records of the fire, including injuries and loss of property involved.

## Finance Director

The leader of the finance department directs and coordinates most all of the finance functions of the organization from purchasing to payroll. He or she is responsible for developing and maintaining the company's financial policies and procedures by providing direction to finance or accounting managers. Particularly in tough budgetary cycles, the finance director determines the financial needs of the municipality as well as the individual departments by keeping executive-level management informed of each department's financial progress and problems.

## Human Resources Director

All institutions or government bodies need personnel to administer and operate the day-to-day activities necessary to achieve their goals. The functions of the city's human resources department, such as hiring, training, and evaluating, are addressed in greater detail in a later chapter of this book. For now, we can simply say that the director of human resources ultimately ensures that all departments treat employees fairly and equitably; that department, city, state, and federal personnel rules and policies are strictly adhered to (such as Equal Opportunity Employment and sexual harassment policies). The director of human resources also directs employee relations and negotiations between management and labor groups.

## Information Technology Director

In today's technology-dependent society, city and government agencies have found it necessary to coordinate the needs, wants, and demands of their organization's internal technology resources. Additionally, they need to ensure that their internal and external networks remain stable, free from outside intrusion and computer viruses, and capable of providing critical services at all times. The information technology director manages these resources for the public agency. Each department, including the library, may have its own computer network, technology operations, and information technology staff, but these resources must all be coordinated into the larger city government operation to safeguard the entire information system. Additionally, the information technology director ensures that computer resources are up to date. He or she must therefore review and evaluate new technology and telecommunication products and trends to recommend hardware or software upgrades from which the agency can benefit.

## Planning Director

Students of public administration have often found it surprising that city or county government officials are strictly bound to how, where, and when their jurisdictions can be physically developed and redeveloped or how housing and businesses within their jurisdiction can be provided and operate. There exists a sort of "blueprint" for development. Most of these decisions are made through a long-range general plan created, approved, and adopted by community individuals and government officials many years before. These general plans consist of statements of policies informing the public on how their communities can be developed. Planning directors oversee general plans and conduct their department's work to ensure that the general plan is followed. They help to develop and set forth standards and general plan proposals, helping the jurisdiction to fine-tune and amend the general plan if possible. In completing their duties, planning directors become very much involved in land use and open-space conservation decisions, housing implementation, traffic circulation, and community code enforcement.

## Public Works Director

A public works department is held accountable for maintaining and operating the public's infrastructure such as garbage collection, water supplies, street maintenance, and public building maintenance. When your library's carpets need to be cleaned, lightbulbs need to be changed, or toilets clog, it is likely the public works department you or your staff will contact to submit a "work order" for maintenance. Heading these departments are public works directors. They review, monitor, and coordinate the successful operation and development of the city's vital services such as streets, garbage, and water. Public works directors assess and evaluate the equipment necessary to provide services, oversee engineering projects, marshal resources necessary to maintain government buildings, and coordinate inspections, construction, replacement, and repairs of community property. Working with the city's engineers and planners, public works directors or their staff members work with developers, contractors, and builders to ensure that projects meet building, plumbing, electrical, and other codes.

## City Attorney

Most any agency providing services to the public at large is exposed to legal matters. Perhaps a city's garbage truck hits a parked car, a police officer's dog bites a citizen, or someone trips on a hole in the sidewalk when approaching the city's library. The city attorney's office will represent the city or government agency, its elected officials and staff, the city's departments, and its individual boards and commissions in the event a lawsuit or complaint is filed against the city. The city attorney's job is to become proactively involved in how services are provided to reduce the risk of a lawsuit. For example, the city attorney's office may evaluate the legal merit of a policy or code to ascertain how the policy would withstand a civil challenge. The city attorney will also help officials and staff members stay clear of potential breaches of established laws by advising them on conducting public meetings or negotiating with employee groups.

## City Clerk

The mere fact that a city operates for the benefit of the entire community's good alludes to the fact that someone must be held accountable as the "keeper" of the city's records, notes, policies, codes, resolutions, ordinances, contracts, and other official records for the public's review. City clerks serve as the central administrators of city records. They ensure that public agendas, meeting notes, and official announcements are distributed. The clerk attends the elected official's public meetings to call roll and record notes. The clerk's vast depository of official documents must be organized, accessible, and made available to the public in an efficient manner. Of particular note, the city clerk implements and coordinates the city's elections to ensure that fair, accurate, and legal voting procedures are followed.

These persons all serve the citizens of the community offering services for their welfare. The public library is a department within the city and is a part of public administration.

# CHAPTER 3

## The Design of an Organization

The notion of the "public good" is continually at the heart of public administrative duties. Because of this, we ask ourselves questions such as, "Am I spending the tax payers' money effectively?" "Am I providing a good return on the public's investment in my organization?" and "Are the services I am offering the ones the public needs, wants, and demands?" Perhaps because of our intense relationship with organizations in our society, one of the initial questions administrators should ask centers around our organization itself, "Is my organization designed and structured appropriately to achieve certain goals and objectives?"

We all participate in some form of organizational structure on a daily basis. Whether at school, work, the doctor's office, or even church, we deal with an organization that has been created by someone to achieve something in a calculated manner for a specific reason. Unfortunately, our notion of organizational structure and design became familiar to so many of us when the perils of bureaucracies, rule-bound institutions, incompetent and uncaring bosses, and insensitivity to customers, permeated popular culture through books, movies, and TV. Our perceptions of "the organization" are therefore tainted somewhat to the point where we may sometimes perpetuate stereotypical ideas about our experiences in them, whether our experiences are real or not. Learning about organizations helps us to ask informed questions about our business practices and their effectiveness. Therefore, understanding organizational design, the benefits of certain institutional structures, and the real potential for inefficiencies inherent to the bureaucratic world should be a primary focus in the study of public library administration.

# What Is an Organization?

Anytime you join two or more people together and ask them to accomplish some predetermined set of goals, you ostensibly have what could be termed an "organization." You are already familiar with big organizations such as Microsoft, Google, and the like. However, you can also classify the local grocery store operated by a father and son as an organization. Organizations range from simple to complex in design. Size has nothing to do with classifying something as an organization. Also, although there is no one best structure for all organizations, there are certain attributes that all organizations need to address. Newly employed librarians and students should understand the typical characteristics that are common to each organization and the questions administrators need to ask that are intrinsic to each characteristic respectively.

1. All organizations must decide *how to divide their work* among the entire organization. This characteristic, sometimes called **job design,** will determine how the organization will divide its objectives into separate parts and how it will assign those parts to positions within the organization.

2. All organizations group various positions into manageable units or departments. This characteristic is called **departmentalization**. Which departments should be held accountable for each objective and what logical groupings will help the organization achieve its objectives effectively?

3. All organizations distribute or delegate **responsibility and authority,** holding those accountable to certain objectives.

4. All organizations establish a **chain of command** to distinguish between positions with direct authority and positions that offer only advisory or support help.

5. All organizations determine the **span of management,** or the number of subordinates who will report to each manager.

# How to Divide Work

Any collection of people faced with accomplishing a complex task is faced with two questions: How will we divide the labor? and How will we coordinate our efforts effectively? In looking at this issue, we are essentially asking about job design. Separating the organization's activities into distinct individual tasks and assigning these to different individuals is sometimes called "job specialization." Job specialization becomes necessary when the organization is simply too large for any one individual to manage.

The organization benefits when an employee has to learn only a specific, highly specialized task because that individual can learn to do it far more quickly and efficiently. The employee does not lose time and effort changing from one operation to another and can concentrate energy on accomplishing that one task. The more specialized the job, the easier it may be to design specialized equipment for those who do it. Additionally, the more specialized the job, the easier it is to train a new employee to replace another employee due to absence.

Job specialization has, of course, some drawbacks which have become problematic in the workplace, most notably employee boredom and job dissatisfaction. Administrators must become aware of these negative consequences and learn to deal with them appropriately. Common solutions to the negative effects of job specialization include job rotation, which is shifting employees from one job to another, and job enlargement, increasing employee responsibilities and accountability.

# Departmentalization

The process by which an organization allocates its people into specific jobs and activities and into more manageable organizational roles is known as departmentalization. Some texts will refer to these basic building blocks as "vertical and horizontal differentiation." These are essentially the same processes of assigning departmentalization to the organization. Generally, departmentalization within libraries is determined by the set of behaviors required of persons in their organizational positions (i.e., children's librarian or acquisitions clerk). However, several other methods of departmentalization may make sense in the business world and are occasionally employed by certain libraries.

1. Departmentalization by function

2. Departmentalization by location

3. Departmentalization by product

4. Departmentalization by customer

## Departmentalization by Function

Organizing departments by the work being done within them—that is, by function—is by far the most common form of organizational design. The popularity of this form of organization departmentalization can be attributed to the fact that it is useful to any type of organization. Many organizations tend to have similar functions such as finance, sales, and marketing, so it isn't surprising to learn that they choose this sort of departmentalization. Most public libraries utilize this functional design approach. In this structure, individuals in each department perform duties that relate to the same organizational activity, circulation services, cataloging, reference, and information technology, among others. More important, departmentalization by function provides the opportunity to obtain efficiencies by consolidating employees with common skills, knowledge, and specialties into common units. However, this sort of departmentalization can lead to problems if employees with these specialized functions become more concerned with their own specialized area than with the operation and mission of the organization as a whole.

## Departmentalization by Location

Another typical form of departmentalization is to group activities completed by employees according to the geographic area in which they are performed. Coca-Cola, for example, groups its sales departments into geographic regions domestically and internationally. This form of departmentalization makes sense for organizations that are spread throughout the world or that have many locations across the United States. Having departments grouped this way may provide better, more responsive customer service because employees can develop an expertise in handling problems specific to one location and gain a better understanding of geographic needs and demands. Unfortunately, this departmentalization design can result in the need to add more complex levels of management to the whole organization to ensure quality control and to coordinate the consistent application of organizational rules and regulations. Some larger public library systems that have many branch libraries with separate staff assigned to these branches spread throughout a large region can be thought of as having set up a hybrid form of departmentalization by location.

## Departmentalization by Product

When an organization has formed departments by grouping together all activities related to a particular product or service, they have utilized a departmentalization by product design. These types of organizations may seem more familiar if you think of your local department store. For example, stores group together employees into the shoe department, cosmetics department, or menswear department, to name a few. Business professionals tend to believe that departmentalization by product allows staff to become more customer-centered and focused around current product trends and demands. Certainly this design offers a great deal of clearly delineated lines of responsibility. Therein lies a good deal of the problems inherent to this type of departmentalization: staff members from individual product lines are not often aware of products and services offered by other departments within the same organization; furthermore, competition across product lines for resources increases.

## Departmentalization by Customer

Some organizations group jobs around the activities performed for common customer needs or types of customers. The assumption here is that customers in some departments will have a common and unique set of problems or needs that can best be met by employees specializing in meeting only those needs. For example, a telecommunications company may group its employees in departments for residential customers or for business customers. A public library looking to encourage greater customer satisfaction among specific key customer groups will find benefits with this sort of design as staff tend to become strong advocates for their specific clientele. To some extent, public libraries use a form of this design if they divide children's services, adult services, or young adult services into separate departments.

This type of organization design has potential pitfalls. Similar to departmentalization by product design, conflict and competition between departments for resources increases significantly as staff lose sight of the organization's entire mission and focus only on their own. Additionally, this design lends itself to a good deal of duplication of effort. For example, a problem faced by one set of customers may also be faced by others. However, departments for both customer sets may not know this and may therefore miss an opportunity to coordinate their problem-solving efforts.

## Responsibility and Authority

Division of labor and the coordination of effort is only a portion of the organization necessary in today's business world. The next major decision in looking at organizational design and effectiveness is to determine how authority and responsibility will be distributed.

Assuming that there are managers and subordinates in the organization, the organization must grant the right to direct or guide the activities of others. This is considered "delegation of authority." Someone who has been delegated the authority to direct someone else's activities has been given the organization's approval to extract some sort of appropriate response from the subordinate that helps the organization attain its goals. The subordinate in a particular position within the organization's structure who has been asked to perform the appropriate task or activity is considered obligated or responsible to see that the task is performed as they have been trained to do. This is considered "delegation of responsibility." In general terms, authority flows from the top of the organization down, and responsibility flows in the opposite direction, from the bottom of the organization up.

## Chain of Command—the Scalar Principle

In the previous section, we discussed lines of authority. This rule that authority flows from the top down through every level of the organization is known as the Scalar Principle. It is more commonly referred to as "the chain of command." In our political system, for example, the president has more authority than the vice president; the vice president has more authority than the secretary of state; the secretary of state has more authority than a U.S. ambassador, and so on. A clear understanding of the fact that an employee from one level in an organization communicates with seniors at the higher levels only through his or her own immediate senior is a necessary tool in the proper administration of any organization.

Students must also recognize that there are various levels of authority in an organization, each with its own power and control. The most common levels are the following:

1.   Authority to inform

2.   Authority to recommend

3.   Authority to report

4.   Full authority

Most employees are given the **authority to inform** a supervisor of various alternatives of work-related actions and activities. However, that employee's superior retains the authority to make decisions in that regard. Higher-level employees may list a series of work-related alternatives along with possible actions and decisions. These employees may also analyze these actions and decisions and make recommendations as to which alternatives are best. These employees are assumed to have the **authority to recommend**. They may not, however, implement the recommended action without first getting approval from a superior. Much of the work done by committees is considered to fall within this authority to recommend area. At the organization's higher levels, an employee may have the authority to implement a particular work-related course of action. However, a full report (**authority to report**) of the action taken, as well as the consequences incurred, must be made to the employee's superior. **Full authority,** which is normally retained at the organization's highest level, grants an employee the authority to act independently and make any decision or implement any course of action without approval from a superior.

# Line versus Staff Positions in the Chain of Command

Public organizations are hierarchical in nature and are notorious for their predictable and occasionally cumbersome chain of command. Authority flows from the top to the bottom, and decision making is passed through the lines of authority as seen on an organization chart, a visual representation of the organization's chain of command. However, a more complex aspect of the chain of command sometimes exists in public administration just as it does in the corporate world, line versus staff positional authority.

Persons who have clear authority within the chain of command and whose positions are recognized in the chain of command are said to be part of the "line management." They make decisions and give orders to their direct subordinates to achieve the organization's goals. Many organizations also create positions that provide support, advice, and expertise to an individual within the chain of command. These persons' authority within the chain of command is not so clearly delineated. They are said to be a part of the "staff management" position. Examples within the public organization could be a staff analyst, an information technology consultant, or an efficiency auditor.

Line managers who have line authority can make decisions and implement procedures that relate to the organization's goals. The staff managers may have authority to make decisions and issue directives about their own areas of expertise, but seldom do they have direct authority over line staff. Instead, staff managers are given advisory authority along with the expectation that line managers will consult them before making decisions. Line managers may perceive that staff managers are a threat to their own authority. Line managers may perceive that staff managers lack their own hands-on experience and institutional knowledge. Staff managers who feel that their recommendations and advice are being ignored become resentful.

At this point, it may be helpful to illustrate the line versus staff conflict using a hypothetical library example. Suppose a library is considering the purchase of a new computerized cataloging system. A line manager prefers one vendor's product because she has been using the vendor's previous product and is comfortable with its operation, ease of use, and technical support. The information technology analyst brought to the library to recommend the best product for the organization has noticed that another vendor's cataloging product offers several new cataloging innovations that may increase productivity and eliminate some cataloging errors. The line manager and staff analyst need to know how to come to a consensus and select a product that is best for everyone. Line managers and staff managers whose authority within the organization are not *explicitly* defined will result in unnecessary organizational conflict and distrust and can often lead lower-level employees to flounder with little direction as higher levels sort out the conflict between line and staff managers.

# Span of Management

The final characteristic common to all organizations is the span of management or the span of control, that is, the number of employees assigned to each manager. Central to this characteristic is the issue of "unity of command," that is, each employee must report to and take orders from only one person. Administrators not only must look at whether employees are reporting to only one manager but whether a single manager can effectively handle the number of subordinates he or she has been assigned. For years, administrators have searched to identify the absolute ideal span of management.

Obviously, there is no ideal number of employees that should report to any one manager. To complicate the matter, the span of management can actually change by departments within the same organization. Rather than focusing on the number of employees assigned to each manager, the organization turns its focus on whether the span of management should be "wide" or "narrow." Additionally, the span of management has a direct role in determining the organization's height, that is, the number of layers or management levels in the organization's hierarchy as displayed on its organizational chart.

## Wide Span of Control

If managers supervise a larger number of employees, they are thought to have a wide span of control. A wide span of control usually translates to fewer levels of management hierarchy on the organization chart. Therefore, organizational communication and information dispersion may be quicker and easier. Also, because fewer management levels can translate to needing fewer managers, there may be some cost efficiencies gained by setting up an organization with a wide span of control.

Before using a wide span of management control, the administrator must ensure that the skills of employees within the organization are high and that employees need less supervision and guidance. By the same token, managers must have the time and skill to control a larger number of employees directly reporting to them.

## Narrow Span of Control

If managers supervise a smaller number of employees, they are thought to have a narrow span of control. Managers with a narrow span of management control can quickly communicate with their own individual employees and share feedback and ideas between them more effectively. The need for management skill and time with smaller numbers of employees tends to be lower with narrow spans of control.

Before using a narrow span of control, administrators must recognize certain facts. In theory, narrow spans of management will require employees to interact more frequently with one another. Consequently, managers may find that they not only must manage their own working relationship with the employees but also the relations between the employees themselves. Narrow spans of management can also create situations in which managers may become too involved in the work of their subordinates, lowering morale and reducing their inclination to be more innovative.

## Centralization versus Decentralization

In considering how authority is delegated throughout an organization, it is important to note how decisions are truly made. If the superiors at the top levels make the organization's key decisions utilizing little or no input from below, then the organization is considered to be "centralized." An organization that assigns decision-making authority to lower levels or that tends to share decision making across the organization is considered to be "decentralized." Decentralization empowers lower-level employees and grants them authority to improve their performance by giving them reporting authority and the ability to act to improve deficient or inefficient areas immediately without approval from the top of the organization.

In principle, neither centralized nor decentralized organizations are perfect in every situation. What works in one situation may not work for another. As potential or newly appointed public administrators, students and librarians must become aware of when a centralized organization may be helpful to their institution and when a decentralized organization may offer improvements to the public. One factor influencing the level of decentralization is the external environment in with the organization operates. For example, those libraries facing or experiencing a financial or environmental crisis may find it advantageous to utilize one source of decision making to lead them effectively—that is, they may choose a centralized organization. However, a library that has been identified as wasteful or inefficient or that has poor-quality service may find advantages in utilizing the skills and expertise of employees on the front lines at lower levels and therefore decentralize its decision-making authority, allowing these employees to make recommendations and implement quality improvement decisions.

## Organizational Charts

Once the organization is designed, people inside and outside of the organization must be able to quickly understand its structure and lines of command. An important administrative tool in illustrating your organization is to present it graphically in the form of an organizational chart. In theory, anyone can understand from whom people in the organization take orders, who reports to whom, and the various departments and unit personnel involved in getting the job of the organization accomplished. The chart displays the organization's hierarchy, and with one quick look, it will show the number of management layers contained within the organization, thereby providing clues to how centralized or decentralized the organization is.

Organization charts typically take on a pyramidal shape. At the tip of this pyramid, they show the organization's leader. Below the leader, the various subordinates are grouped, usually in progressively smaller boxes. Peers within the organization generally have boxes of similar size on an organizational chart. For example, in a library that has three senior librarians supervising units, these positions would each appear on the same horizontal line, in three separate boxes of identical size.

The typical chart shows all the organization's positions or "boxes" connected by a series of lines intended to convey the relationships between positions both above and below them. Although these series of lines become complex and confusing with larger organizations, there are some commonalities. In general, solid lines depict a direct, formal working relationship between positions. A dotted or dashed line indicates an advisory or indirect relationship between positions. Because many organizations are continually growing, shrinking, or changing in some way, the organization's chart needs to be continually updated. For this reason, many charts are now created online to facilitate quick and easy restructuring and redesign.

Once the organization has been structured, the next step is to understand the power and politics in an organization. This is discussed in the next chapter.

# CHAPTER 4

## Power and Politics in Organizations

In the previous chapter, we discussed the design and structure of the organization. Public administrators strive to create their organizations to reflect these "ideals." We must remember, however, that organizations are dynamic. They change and function under certain environmental and situational pressures that can, and often do, influence the ways in which the organization operates. These intrinsic elements sometimes seem to make the organization operate in ways that defy the organization chart. *Organizational charts don't account for, or even explain, how two organizational behaviors, power and politics, affect the whole.* Occasionally, accountability is lost, the chain of command breaks down, or decisions are made at a level without the legitimate authority to make that decision. Informal networks can form outside formal channels, and staff may employ nonformal means of collaboration to solve complex organizational issues. For example, you may call your friend in the city's human resources department to kick around an idea you have regarding restructuring your library's work team. This certainly seems easier than approaching your direct boss to arrange a meeting and discuss the issue. Additionally, charts and design do not address *who* gets important resources and how these resources are allocated. In this chapter, I discuss the sometimes invisible, but equally important, role that power and politics play in organizational behavior and operations.

## Why Study Power

Power is one of the most important dynamics of an organization. An understanding of what power is and the processes of power is important in determining not only *how* organizations work but *why* they work. With an element as important to the workings of the organization, it sometimes surprises new library directors and students that there is hesitancy to discuss power in the context of public administration. Discussing power often brings up connotations of dishonesty, backstabbing, hidden agendas, or corruption. However, consider an organization in which nobody had power. Would the organization get anything done, and if it did, how? The important concept to remember about power is that if it is not identified and controlled within the organization, its potential misuse can cause dysfunction and confusion. Leaders and managers within the organization may sometimes attempt to exercise power for their own benefit or to accomplish goals contrary to the will of the public. For this reason, students in public administration should understand what power is, how it is acquired, and the proper ways in which to use it.

## What Is Power?

To understand what power means when discussing it in the context of an organization, students should visualize a model in which Person A wants Person B to behave in a certain way. Person A cannot make Person B do something unless Person B wants to do it. The act of getting Person B to *want* to do something he or she would not normally do is the act of exerting power. Power in organizations tends to follow this model, i.e., one person attempting to change the behavior of one or more individuals, particularly if these other individuals would not have changed their behavior otherwise.

In looking at the model of power in this way, you will notice that there exists an implied resistance that the person wishing to change the other's behavior (Person A) must overcome. The normal assumption seems to be that, in the organization, the power Person A has can be derived from the organization's structure, that is, through the legitimate lines vested by the organization's hierarchy. The higher the position Person A has within the structure, the greater his or her base of power will be in accessing the resources necessary to overcome the resistance of Person B. Although this is certainly true in many occasions, power does not always follow this rule.

# Power versus Authority

Before proceeding with an examination of the role of power within the organization, it is necessary to make an important distinction. Students sometimes make the mistake of assuming that a person who exerts power over someone else has the authority to exert that power. The model of power just discussed does *not* imply a person's right to exert that power. Person A may have the *ability* to influence Person B's behavior even though Person A may or may not have the right, or authority, to do so. The *authority* to expect Person B to behave in a particular way or comply with the exertion of power exists within the organization's chain of command. If Person A is Person B's boss, than Person A has the legitimate positional authority to secure compliance from Person B to behave in a certain way. However, Person A may still secure compliance from Person B to perform certain actions even if Person A does not have the positional authority to expect such action. Grasping the difference between power and authority will assist you in understanding the organization's informal operations that exist outside its command structure and design.

To illustrate this important difference between power and authority, the following example may be helpful. A library branch manager has required that his or her children's librarian coordinate a summer reading program for the community. Presumably, the branch manager has the positional authority, the right, to require the children's librarian, who is subordinate, to perform this duty as it would normally fall within the job's responsibilities. This same branch librarian probably does not have the authority to require the children's librarian to mow the lawn in front of the library. However, the children's librarian may well agree to mow the lawn if the branch manager has the ability to influence the librarian's behavior by exerting some sort of power—perhaps an offer of time off, the promise of a pay increase, or possible punishment. Obviously, for purposes of illustration, this example provides an oversimplification of the relationship between the manager and the subordinate. However, the important lesson is to understand that power and authority exist within a different realm of organizational behavior and that power can account for unexpected performance both good and bad.

# Dependency Theory of Power

Before discussing the means by which power can be acquired in an organization, it is useful to examine more closely the role of resistance we identified in the model of power discussed in the previous section. If the successful use of power equates to one's ability to exact a certain behavior from someone by overcoming resistance from someone who would otherwise not perform that action, how do leaders in organizations overcome this resistance? What we are really asking here is, "Why do employees respond to someone else's exertion of power?" The answer lies in the dependency theory of power.

The dependency theory of power states that, within the model of power we have discussed, Person A and Person B must share a dependency on one another for the exertion of power to be useful and successful. In particular, for Person A to exert power successfully, he or she must possess certain resources that Person B needs. These resources must be important, scarce, and non-substitutable. For example, if Person B needs money, and if Person A is in a role to dispense money, then Person B will likely be receptive to Person A's influence of power. If promotions within the organization are rare, and Person B perceives an opportunity to be promoted by Person A, Person B will believe that Person A has control over a scarce resource, that is, promotions. Person B will therefore be receptive to Person A's influence of power. Finally, if Person B needs a specific desired resource unavailable from anyone else, perhaps time off of the schedule, and Person A can claim that she is the sole person who can approve time off requests, then Person B will likely be receptive to Person A's exertion of power.

Dependency works both ways, and in public administration, it is quite useful to visualize the power relationship existing between two parties in this way. In so doing, we begin to understand that power plays a reciprocal role in this dependency model. Obviously both parties may have resources the other needs to complete the organization's mission. For example, Person B may have important skills, knowledge, or abilities that Person A needs to fulfill his or her department's role in the organization successfully. Each of these parties controls some resource that the other party needs. In an ideal world, the dependency relationship between Person A and Person B would be balanced, and cooperation would be prevalent within the organization. However, let's consider the more typical responses to power that exist between the two parties.

In one extreme, Person A has significant power over Person B, and there is no reciprocal relationship. Person B's dependency on Person A for all the important, scarce, and non-substitutable resources is supreme. In this case, Person A could expect that Person B would comply with all of his or her exertion of power. In this case, the response to power is *compliance*.

If, however, Person B holds a resource that Person A needs at a particular time, Person B may attempt to negotiate with Person A's attempt to exert power. For example, if the library branch manager asked a part-time librarian to work overtime to cover scheduling problems, that librarian might attempt to negotiate some time off at a future date in return. Obviously, the branch manager still holds the balance of power (he or she sets schedules). However, because he or she needs the librarian to work to cover a scheduling emergency, the librarian holds a desired resource, and the librarian has an elevated degree of power allowing him or her to negotiate. In this case, the response to power is to *bargain*.

In some cases, Person B may have more power than Person A. In this case, Person B may respond to Person A's attempt to exert power by resisting it. If, for example, the library's computer system has suddenly crashed, there would be no one more powerful than the information technology staff member assigned to fix the problem. No matter how important Person A at the library thinks he or she is, if the information technology staff member does not see the job as a priority, he or she may resist attempts to get the library's computer fixed before someone else's. Because the information technology person has the complete power (skill and expertise), in this case the response to power could very well be to *fight*.

Finally, in some rare cases, Person B may have absolute power. Certainly this scenario is more likely to occur in the public realm than most any other type of organization. As an example, consider a city government in fiscal crisis that has required all departments to cut their budgets by 15 percent. The police officers' union, which has contributed a substantial amount of money to the political campaigns of three of the five ruling city council members, may choose to ignore the police chief's attempt to get the union to agree to eliminate employee benefits in their department. The response to power in this case is to *ignore*.

## How Is Power Acquired?

We have already identified one of the typical means through which power can be acquired in an organization, that is, power that comes with a position within the organization's chain of command. The idea here is that the higher one rests in the organization's levels of supervision, the more power that person would have and the more legitimate is that person's exertion of power. Power holders with positional power within the organization claim a legal and rational obedience on the grounds that their orders fall within the scope of their office or position. There are other positional bases of power, and although they do not necessarily affect a great deal of positions within the public realm, they do occur from time to time.

Some power is acquired merely from the traditional or customary means through which the position is filled. For example, kings and queens ascend to power by claiming they have divine right or that their family has control of the crown. The sanctity of custom or sacred tradition has given them power. In local government, particularly in smaller communities, council members or town leaders often win elections and acquire substantial power simply because their family has been in the community for many decades. Their father, and their father's father, was the mayor many years ago, and the traditional base of power is then passed along to their sons or daughters. Public administrators are keenly aware of whose families have been in the community a long time to help them understand where power is likely to rest within the government's structure.

Some power comes from a person's ability within a position to dole out rewards (whether monetary or not), particularly if rewards are tied to performance. For example, the library school instructor who assigns grades to students and who thereby determines who graduates and who does not holds a substantial degree of positional reward power over students in his or her class. If students want to graduate, they will strive to perform well enough to exact a high grade as a form of reward from the instructor.

The flip side of reward power is coercive power. If a person's position provides the capacity to dole out punishment, he or she has acquired positional coercive power. Leaders who have coercive power as a part of their position can exert their ability (regardless if that ability is real or only implied) to fire, demote, transfer to an undesirable position, or strip away a subordinate's benefits.

## Other Means of Power

The power bases described above are positional-based power because they are acquired as a result of a person's position within the organization's structure. Sometimes power can be acquired through means outside of the formal structure. These are often described as personal power bases.

Personal power bases are often tied to the connection with an individual's particular personal quality. Charismatic power, sometimes called "referent power," is acquired by an individual's ability to attract admiration and respect through charismatic charm and persona. Mahatma Gandhi, John F. Kennedy, and religious prophets are considered extraordinary examples of leaders who had the ability to exert power as a result of their personal charisma. Modern-day advertisers often employ charismatic or referent power techniques by using celebrity endorsements to sell products. An individual who admires and respects Michael Jordan, for example, would likely choose to buy a certain brand of shoes if Jordan were to endorse it on television or in print advertisements.

Expert power can be an extremely potent base of personal power for individuals within the organization. An individual who holds superior skills and abilities critical to the organization's success should be considered to possess expert power. As discussed earlier, when your computer breaks down, the information technology person sent to fix your computer has an inordinate amount of personal power.

# Responses to Power

When exerting power to exact a desired behavior, the probable and expected response would be one of three: resistance, compliance, or commitment. The positional (legitimate, traditional, reward, and coercive) and personal (charismatic and expert) bases of power discussed earlier seem to result in varying degrees of compliance. Of all the positional power bases, coercive power would exact the least amount of cooperation and in fact may result in a high level of resistance. Reward, legitimate, and traditional power tend to result in compliance (although a dependency relationship between Person A and Person B will likely affect the rate of compliance). However, personal power bases and the exertion of charismatic and expert power have proven to result in much higher levels of commitment than any other.

# Organizational Politics Defined

Having power and the ability to use it is one thing. Using power to attain favorable outcomes must involve a programmatic use of processes that will increase the probability that you, your colleagues, your department, your coalition, and others will gain the resources you want, need, or demand, whatever those resources may be. The activity or process of actually using that power to pursue one's own agenda or self-interests is the topic of this section. Within an ideal organization, there would be no opposition. Employers could expect employees to perform their duties without the need to exert any power. If there is no opposition, there is no need to exert power.

Within any organization, however, staff members bring their own interests, needs, wants, and desires to the workplace. More likely than not, these interests tend to conflict with the needs, wants, and desires of others within the organization, if not the organization's mission itself. In government bodies, these conflicting interests typically involve competition for limited resources. Organizations need processes in which conflicting interests among departments, units, or employees can be reconciled. We can define organizational politics as those actions taken within an organization to reconcile competing interests such as the use of one's positional or personal power.

Because of the scarcity of resources, ambiguous organizational goals, and constant environmental change within the institution, organizations are more likely to rely on political activity than any other formal means of influence to make decisions and solve problems. Within this context, power relations between the organization's employees come into play. Is the political activity originating inside or outside of the organization? Is the attempted political influence occurring between employees at the same level within the hierarchy or between higher and lower levels? Finally, how is the political action sanctioned or legitimized by the organization? By asking these questions and attempting to understand the organization's power relations, we have begun to focus on the tactics staff members employ in their attempts to influence the political process.

# Political Tactics

Because many organizational decisions are made through the use of politics, successful public administrators look for ways to increase the influence of their power. This requires utilizing certain skills and abilities that will get the outcomes public administrators want. Quite a few tactics may be used in attempting to influence organization politics. Most are based on interpersonal power relations—power used between persons within the interpersonal communication process. A few other tactics revolve around using the power of information. This section identifies some of the more common political tactics used within the organization.

## Interpersonal-Based Political Tactics

### Gatekeeping

Gatekeepers decide who and what gets passed through the organization's chain of command. They also control when it can get passed through. In particular, the organization gatekeeper controls access to key persons. A common political tactic is to influence the gatekeeper to gain critical access to individuals the gatekeeper "controls." As an example, consider city managers of city governments. They are the busiest individuals in the organization, with constant meetings with individuals and groups. The city manager typically employs an executive secretary who controls the manager's schedule and daily meetings. The library director who wants to meet with the city manager must compete for his or her attention with the police chief, fire chief, city council meetings, developers, and others. To gain access to the city manager, the library director decides to frequently purchase flowers for, or bring goodies to, the manager's secretary in hopes that the secretary will "open the gate" and let the library director through when requested to be let through.

### Attacking or Blaming Others

A common tactic most parents are familiar with is the attempt to influence a decision or distract someone from your own faults by blaming someone else for theirs. This tactic is employed by individuals who need to stabilize their power and therefore tear down someone else's. For example, a fire chief attempts to make less of his involvement in a poor decision by saying he or she was lied to by the planning director.

### Forming Power Coalitions with Strong Allies

Numbers have power, especially when those numbers include individuals who are considered powerful. A strong political tactic is to attempt to influence one's own power in getting interests met by enlisting the help of others within the organization who are seen as influential. As an example, a library director who wants to hire a security officer for the library attempts to enlist the support of the police chief, the county sheriff, and the local Parent Teacher Association.

### Creating Obligations

Those who wish to create a powerful coalition or influence a decision in their own favor often employ this "You scratch my back and I'll scratch yours" tactic. These individuals hope to gain the support for their own interest by promising to do the same for another person when needed. This tactic of reciprocity has fairly significant political uncertainty to it because one never knows what reciprocal favor might be asked in return.

## Informational-Based Political Tactics

### Logical Arguments and Factual Evidence

It is hard to argue with the facts, and the best and most effective political tactic used in public administration is the presentation of factual evidence. Finding information that supports your interests and presenting the information in a logical and rational fashion will increase your ability to sway decisions. It is an effective means of increasing your own power without attempting to undermine that of someone else.

### Distorting or Withholding Information

A common political tactic is to withhold important information that might be necessary to make an informative decision. Another tactic that seems far more sinister is to attempt to distort the information that *is* made available so that the decision made favors a particular interest. For instance, a library director wishing to present a favorable picture of the library's increasing checkout rate gathers last year's numbers and compares them to this year's. The director shows that this year's numbers are 25 percent higher than last year, meaning people are checking out more items. What the director neglected to show was that the library was closed for three weeks the previous year because of some renovations. A "per day" checkout rate shows that, on average, the library checkout rate had actually decreased slightly.

### Overwhelming Others with Information

Sometimes presenting too much information can confuse and overwhelm the person or persons making a decision. With an overwhelming amount of information to consider, the hope is that a decision will defer to the individual who has presented to most information, even if that information cannot be understood or processed effectively.

### Controlling the Agenda

Much like the gatekeeper, the political tactic of controlling the agenda is an effective tool in public administration. Decisions in the public realm can rarely be made in private. City councils or local government entities can rarely act on items that have not first been publicly noticed. The public must be made aware of the fact a decision will be made on a particular issue. Typically, this is done by posting a public agenda. The person who controls what is placed on the agenda, often the city manager, the mayor, or both, has the potential to use a significant political tactic in the decision making process.

## Conclusion

As you have perhaps noticed, politics, and the use of influencing tactics, is sometimes referred to as "power plays." Using power as a means to influence decisions that benefit your or your department's or unit's interests occurs quite frequently outside the formal framework of the organization. It should be noted that, in general, the use of politics to accomplish goals should not be considered good or bad. Some of the means or tactics utilized need to be scrutinized. Politics may be legitimately used and sanctioned within the organizational framework (logical arguments and factual evidence) or illegitimately used and going beyond the organization's sanctioned limits (distorting information). The choice of which tactic, or power play, to use would certainly depend on the personal interests and motives, personality factors, and the current work environment involved. Our goal in public administration is to prevent the use of politics in such a way that it consumes unnecessary time, creates unnecessary tension, or disrupts the will of the public and diminishes the trust the public has placed on us to serve the common good rather than our own personal interests.

# CHAPTER 5

# Budgeting

Public administrators spend a part of each day working with and worrying about budget needs. It is easy to think of the budget in terms of matching fund allocations to each department's mission and objectives—thinking in terms of "this is what the city needs from my department, this is how our department intends to fulfill that need, so this is the amount of money it needs." However, the process is far more complex for the public administrator. This chapter presents information on budgeting, types of public agency budgets, and methods for presenting budget data.

## Budgets in the Public World

Each local government or public authority is required by law to establish and maintain an accounting system. The accounting system is designed to show, in detail, the assets, revenues, and expenses of the local government. The system chosen represents what is most commonly referred to as "the budget." It is important to look at the budget as a public document. The public entrusts its administrators with a serious duty. They ask that public administrators spend the money collected through taxes, revenue, and fees in a wise and responsible manner. They expect that the public's money will be used to fund relevant services and provide those services in cost-efficient and -effective ways. They also ask that administrators remain legally accountable for the money obtained from the public. Public administrators must be able to reassure the public in some way that the money has indeed been spent in logical, rational, and responsible ways. So how do public administrators do this?

Public administrators reassure the public by developing a spending plan, also known as an operating budget. Like the budgets we prepare for ourselves at home, a budget is simply a plan of how much will be spent and on what. It is a public document, visible to anyone. The budget construction process will normally follow the organizational chart. Each component of the entity will be involved in preparing budget information relative to its unit. This information is successively compiled together as it is passed up through the organization until an overall budget plan is achieved. However, beyond the data compilation, there are critical differences in how budgets are actually developed among different organizations. Some entities follow a top-down, or mandated approach. Others utilize a bottom-up, or participative philosophy.

## Constructing a Budget

Before delving into specifics about the budget construction cycle, we can simplify the process by looking at it in broad terms. The construction process normally follows the organizational chart. Personnel of the local government, particularly those in management positions, will be directly or indirectly involved in preparing their unit's budget information. Once the information has been created at these smaller unit levels, it is sent to a central location within the department. It is compiled together as it is passed up through the organization's chart so that the one overall budget plan is created.

In general, we should look at public administration budgeting as being directed from the top down, and most local government organizations will follow a top-down mandated approach to budgeting. These budgets begin with those at the top of the organizational chart, top-level management, establishing either general or specific parameters under which the budget is to be prepared. These parameters usually come down in the form of a "budget message" from the chief executive instructing other managers to submit budget proposals outlining what their goals and objectives for the next fiscal year will be. The lower one goes in the organizational chart, the lower the likelihood of personnel having input in setting or shaping this budget proposal. Managers and personnel at the mid-levels of the organization chart may influence the process by communicating their unit needs, specific statistical analysis, priorities, and data about trends up to top-level managers, but for the most part, top-level management imposes budget directives down from top to bottom.

# Where Does the Money Come From?

In general, a good deal of the money cities and other local government spend is generated by local taxes and fees. One of the largest portions of local government revenue comes in the form of federal and state "intergovernmental transfers." The most common of these are what are known as "categorical grants" that larger government agencies dole out to jurisdictions to support certain services and programs. These grants provide funding for specific programs such as housing, social services, education, transportation, and community development and cannot be used for any other purposes.

Property taxes also account for one of the largest revenue generators for local governments. Property taxes are paid to the local jurisdiction by all persons who own property within that local jurisdiction. These taxes vary from city to city and from state to state, but they are often based on a formula related to a percentage of the fair market value of the property one owns. Other local government revenue sources include fees and charges such as overdue library material fines, fees for refuse collection and water provision, and sales tax.

# Where Does the Money Go?

Once collected, all of the revenue generated via grants, taxes, fees and charges go into one of the jurisdiction's many "funds" through which the revenues can then be allocated and distributed. A fund is a separate fiscal and accounting entity with its own self-balancing set of accounts; its own assets, liabilities, and equity; and its own revenues and expenditures. Each local government or public authority establishes and maintains in its budget or accounting system many types of funds. The following are examples of some of the more common funds with which a public administrator, including library administrators, should be familiar. The generic meaning of each type of fund listed in the following subsections (general, enterprise, and capital projects) is usually determined by general accounting principles and standards.

## The General Fund

The largest fund in most cities is what is called the "general fund." Unlike some of the other funds you will learn about in this chapter, the general fund is the city's primary funding source and generally has few, if any, funding restrictions. The general fund portion of the jurisdiction's budget is used to support most all of the general municipal services, including police, fire, streets, parks, libraries, planning, and community and economic development. We will discuss establishing a department budget in greater detail later in this chapter. For now it is fine just to understand that typically money from the whole general fund is allocated to each department in response to that department's spending plan proposal. When administrators talk about budget cuts, reductions in revenue, and most spending transactions, they are more than likely referring to this critical funding source.

For public libraries, a large portion of our operating funds are allocated from the local government's general fund. For example, expenditures for materials, staffing, utilities, and programming normally are charged to the general fund. It is not uncommon to see libraries funded at 95 percent or more by the local government's general fund. However, the portion of the whole general fund pie allocated to public libraries is normally very small. Therefore, when challenged to reduce its operating budget, even if only by a small percentage, the overall effect for the library can be devastating. Further complicating the matter is that most of the general fund revenue public libraries receive is used to pay the salary and benefits of our library staff. So again, when asked to reduce its operating budget, libraries find it difficult to avoid reducing anything other than staff in order to meet a reduction target.

## Enterprise Funds

Local government jurisdictions offer services that are commercial in nature, providing some goods or services to the public for a cost. The theory is that the charge is levied so that the service can by self-supporting. In reality, however, most cities charge a fee large enough that any money gathered in excess of the cost of providing the service is placed into a special fund, known as an "enterprise fund." Examples of enterprise fund generators would be refuse collection and water or utility provision. Enterprise funds are used to pay for the cost of providing the service at large as well as to expand or improve the service in the future. For example, if the refuse unit needs to purchase a new garbage truck or replace refuse containers, the money would come from the enterprise fund through which the service operates.

Having enterprise funds gives communities some flexibility to account separately for the finances and transactions associated with a broad range of municipal services. Revenues and expenses of the services provided through these funds are segregated into their own financial statements separate from the general fund and all other governmental activities. This is not to say that these funds do not come without restrictions on using them. Quite the opposite is true, in fact. Because many enterprise funds draw matching federal, state, and grant dollars each year, which go into dozens of contracts with local companies, use of the funds for specific projects and specific expenses are typical. A community may not establish enterprise funds for "normal" operations or services offered by local government, such as public safety. As stated above, most enterprise funds must show that they are funding the direct costs of providing the service for which the enterprise fund was established.

The American Library Association and the Library Bill of Rights propose that library services be made accessible free of charge. Enterprise funds seem contrary to that ideal and are therefore somewhat rare within the public library world. Although perhaps not as common as other funds, some libraries do maintain a library enterprise fund. A good example is a library that operates its own café or copy service within the facility. Goods and services sold through these services, theoretically, are sold to maintain the solvency and operation of the service as a courtesy to library customers. Additional funds generated by the services could be used specifically for library purposes if the enterprise fund is restricted to the library separately.

## Capital Projects Fund

A capital projects fund is set up to account for the proceeds, revenue, and expenditures of resources used for the capital projects such as planned construction, repair, and replacement or remodeling of facilities. Many library budgets and those of other city departments as well will show a capital project fund which has been created for a specified project such as expanding or remodeling the Teen Room or Children's Services room. Perhaps a new branch library is to be built, or the heating/air conditioning in an older building needs to be replaced. A capital project fund would be built into the budget to account for that project and track its finance activity outside the financial activity of the general fund.

## Transfers between Funds

Many local government entities strapped for cash or with extreme budget challenges look for alternative sources of revenue to take the pressure off the general fund and support normal operations and services. A common question is, "Can't local governments just take funds from one or more enterprise funds to 'enhance' the general fund?" Because different states and local jurisdictions adopt their own rules and accounting standards, the answer to that question is complex. Depending on the amount of revenue generated by the enterprise activity and the specific public enterprise service from which the revenue was derived, there is opportunity to take money from an enterprise fund to support the general fund. In general, however, cities try to keep the different funds separate. There are many examples, however, of appropriate instances when a local government can justify moving funds from one account to the other. In making the determination on whether funds can be moved, the public administrator must first consider any limitations on the use of the public enterprise revenue. If there are restrictions, does the proposed transfer of funds break any rules? As an example, the use of water revenue enterprise funds may have no explicit restrictions, but use of solid waste enterprise fund revenue could be restricted for use only to support solid waste services or projects. Therefore, using these enterprise funds to, say, pay for a collection of library books would not be legal. The most common type of transfers from an enterprise to the general fund comes when the local jurisdiction is "reimbursing" the general or other fund for subsidizing certain costs of the enterprise.

## Operating versus Capital Budgets

So far we have discussed specific pieces (funds) of a larger pie (a budget). Local governments are required to publish the organization's budget as a public document. When so doing, they will usually produce two (if not more) budgets: an operating budget and a capital budget. These budgets are yearly financial plans that estimate revenue and expenditures for the organization. The revenue section normally details all the projected sources of income the organization expects such as grants, fees, and so forth. The expenditures section typically will detail all of the costs associated with operating the organization such as personnel, supplies, and program expenses.

Capital budgets reflect funds set aside to complete all the capital projects such as building acquisition, remodeling, or construction the organization expects to undertake. Because major capital projects can often take several years to complete, capital budgets are sometimes created once every few years rather than every year like the operating budget. Public administrators consider the operating budget the annual "day-to-day" accounting system of the organization. As such, much more attention in the public administration field is paid to operating budgets than other budgets.

## The Budget Cycle

Most local government organizations use what is known as a "fiscal year" budget cycle rather than a calendar year cycle. For most public agencies, a fiscal year consists of a twelve-month accounting period which usually begins on July 1 and ends on June 30 of the following year. Because a fiscal year spans months from two years, it can sometimes be confusing knowing which month or year to refer to when making reports and presentations. A good rule to consider is that a fiscal year is designated by the year in which it ends. For example, Fiscal Year 2010 ended on the last day in June 2010 and began on July 1, 2009.

Public administrators, including library directors, are never really finished with their budget responsibilities. However, the amount of attention and focus spent on budget preparation is usually determined by the "budget cycle" in effect within the city. The budget cycle is a sequence of events covering the enter life of a budget from beginning to end and then repeats itself for each subsequent fiscal year. The cycle usually begins with the city manager's review of prior year accomplishments and a consideration of what future initiatives must be completed. This review is provided to the local elected officials along with the findings of an independent audit of the organization's entire financial accounting system.

Following is a snapshot of the average budget cycle for local governments. Obviously, each individual city or town has its own calendar and sequence of events that may deviate slightly from this picture, but for the most part this summary typifies the likely chain of events.

## Late Fall/Early Winter

On a city-wide level, the city manager, along with department heads (including the library director and managers), review the fiscal year's accomplishments, expenditures, and unmet needs as they begin to identify future initiatives for the city council to consider during goal setting and strategic planning sessions. The elected officials and city administrators review (and perhaps change) the city's current vision and mission statements. Strategic plans for the next few years are discussed and top priorities for the entire organization are determined for the upcoming fiscal year.

Concurrently, library administrators begin to gather their teams and determine, at the department level, the total financial resources necessary for what the library and the library board or commission expect to accomplish in the future. One of the major challenges for directors and administrators is determining how to handle budgets that continue to grow year after year. Quite often, the department has identified that additional funds are necessary because of higher costs such as maintenance contracts, database licensing, or staff benefits. Additionally, a new service may be up for consideration. The library team begins to construct a proposal that can account for new funding needs. Often this means shifting resources from one fund to another, or increasing funding in one area and decreasing funds in another area may be required. The library administrator and his or her team will project anticipated revenues and begin fine-tuning the department's budget request.

Most public libraries require approval from the library's advisory or governing board before it is passed on to the city council and city manager for approval. You and other library staff members prepare draft budget documents for your board or commission. The trustees will then review the draft budget with the director, propose changes, and complete the board's own process of approving the department budget once they are satisfied with it. Once approved, the department budget is passed on to the city for incorporation into the city's budget, and it eventually awaits the city budget process cycle to complete.

## Late Fall

The city manager and finance manager begin to develop projections for revenue and expenses for the upcoming year. Given the situation of the local, state, and federal economy, a determination is made by the finance team of just how much money individual funds are likely to have available for the next budget year. Using this information, the city manager prepares a budget message for the city, which provides instructions for departments as they begin to prepare individual budget requests. For example, if the finance department has detected that local property tax revenue will be down by a certain percentage, the city manager will pass this information down to city departments via the budget message and instruct that department budgets take this decrease into account, perhaps even specifying the need to reduce department budgets by a certain percentage to compensate for the reduction in revenues.

With this message and budget instruction in hand, department heads then prepare their operating costs (e.g., "We need this much for staffing, this much for collections . . . etc.") and capital project needs (e.g., "We need to re-carpet the library.") in the form of a budget request, or proposal, for the city manager's review. In many cases, budget meetings between the city manager and department heads take place to help refine budget requests before they are officially submitted for approval. These budget meetings are opportunities for the city manager and the public administrator to discuss department budgets and explain certain requests in the proposal and to help each understand the unique needs of the department as they relate to the budget as a whole.

## December

After hearing each of the department's budget requests, and after refining these individual budgets as a team, the city manager and finance director normally will analyze, review, and balance capital and operating budget requests, preparing their final budget recommendations. Because a local government is using public funds to operate, the budgets must be approved and adopted by the elected officials before any money can be spent.

## Early Spring

The city manager presents his or her budget recommendations to the city council or other governing body. In an effort to include citizens and stakeholders in the process, the local government will likely hold public meetings to review recommended budgets by department. Quite often, the council members are given an opportunity to question department heads regarding line items in their budgets or ask that further "refinement" take place. The public is also allowed input and the opportunity to ask questions regarding preliminary budget recommendations. At this point, the public can object to certain items such as service cutbacks or offer support for capital project recommendations such as new library facilities. Because each department is given hearing from the council in regards to the budget proposals submitted, the public comment period can span several weeks.

## Late Spring

The last of the public meetings concludes, and the managers take specific instructions from the city manager to incorporate any last-minute changes to their individual budget requests. It must be remembered that many budgets are discussed at the same time, and participants can become confused as to which funds and which budgets are being discussed; it is always advisable to have a clear understanding of your department budget and your budget submittals before the public input process begins. Not understanding your submittals, or offering inaccurate numbers, can present a negative image to the city manager, the city council, and, worst of all, the public.

## Early Summer

Once the manager has the final draft budgets and departments have incorporated all the changes and counter-changes into their submittals, he or she is ready to take the budget to the city council for final approval and adoption. After this is complete, the elected body will ask that the newly adopted budget be certified in compliance with set state laws. Funds are then ready to be made available to the departments at the start of the next fiscal year.

## Midyear Budget Review

The organization's finance director constantly reviews spending targets and budgeted revenues/expenses throughout the year with the intent of ensuring that projections and estimates are on target and that anticipated revenue is indeed materializing. He or she may recommend midyear adjustments to account for revenue shortfalls or enhancements and to more accurately reflect changes in anticipated revenues and expenses for the fiscal year ending June 30. The elected body must review and approve an amended fiscal year budget, and city staff must certify any budget changes or amendments before the adoption of the next fiscal year budget.

# Actors in the Public Budgeting Process

Those unfamiliar with public budgeting often wonder who the important "players" or "actors" are in the process of planning, preparing, and implementing the local government's budget. The chief executive or city manager obviously holds a top spot in the process, as well as a great deal of the power in constructing the budget. He or she decides the projects and programs that best match the organization's priorities to move forward. The top executive also ultimately decides which funds and allocations will go where after negotiating with the department heads and what the final budget submittal to the council will look like. I have known many a library director (and other department heads) who have thought that their own department budget proposals were decided, only to find that the city manager "adjusted" their proposals prior to putting the submittal forward to the council.

The city council also must be considered a major player in the budgeting process. The council members take the city manager's submittal and can give it a "thumbs up" as is, or they may decide to send it back for more work. Remember, council members are elected officials. They may have made campaign promises or have hidden agendas that they believe are not reflected in the budget as submitted by the city manager for approval. They may request that changes be made before they will approve adopting it. If enough other council members agree, the budget will need to be changed. As an example, one local government had three individuals elected to its city council who were working as public safety officers in other cities. When the city manager submitted a budget that reflected an across-the-board reduction of each department's budgets by 10 percent to close a budget shortfall, the three council members (who arguably had a personal bias favoring public safety) grouped together to exempt the city's police and fire departments from the cut, thereby passing on further and deeper cuts to the city's other departments.

Department heads, particularly the finance director, are critical in the budget cycle process. If a department head is not able and ready to defend budget proposals, it is likely the department budget will be changed. The department head is the one individual who puts forward the direction the department intends to go using the money it hopes to obtain. Department heads must understand their department's budget to respond to questions from each of the other major players. It is essential that they have gathered and analyzed the statistical data necessary to communicate what was accomplished with budget funds the previous fiscal year, what is being considered for funding this fiscal year, and why certain things are being proposed.

The finance director, who has financial data, projections, and estimates, must be considered a key participant and partner in the budget cycle. Library directors can and should take advantage of the financial knowledge the finance director can share. The finance director has a fairly good understanding of each department's budget and can therefore help guide other department heads to craft a department budget submittal that will be more likely to pass muster.

Finally, every public administrator must understand and accept that the citizens of the local government are ultimately key players in the budget cycle. The fact that the organization is using public monies to finance the services and programs we offer cannot be lost on our budget decision and planning process. In the public library world, the "give 'em what they want versus give 'em what they need" argument, so familiar to collection developers, sounds even more relevant when applied to public budgeting.

When creating our department budgets, public administrators must look at how past use of our services is likely to predict future use. How are we accommodating our user wants and demands in the budgets we set forth? If we cannot assure the public that we value their input in the services we offer, how can we justify submitting a budget to use the public's money to offer those same services?

## Budget Committees

Earlier in this discussion, we discussed the fact that public administration often utilizes a top-down budget mandate system in which budget directives are sent down through the organization with little, if any, opportunity for lower-level personnel to have input. The disadvantage of this implementation strategy is that there is little buy-in or ownership of budget objectives by lower levels of the organization. The dictatorial nature of that process leaves little opportunity for innovation and creativity at the bottom of the organization chart. Consequently, many organizations have instituted budget committees in which representatives from each unit are included in the budget planning process. Such a process does allow a far more extensive and valuable amount of feedback and insight about all organizational aspects.

With representation from all levels and ranges within the organization, information relative to individual units, departments, and sections is likely to be brought forward for consideration and advocates for perhaps unseen opportunities and resource needs can be discovered. Far more advantageous to using the budget committee process is the buy-in and ownership of budget decisions and the likelihood that objectives and goals will be met at all levels. However, the budget committee process does not come without any drawbacks. Upper-level management must be able to trust that the committee will make recommendations that benefit the organization as a whole and be ready to incorporate the committee's recommendations into the ultimate budget submittal. If the committee's recommendation doesn't follow the recommendation of the top-level manager, it cannot be simply tossed aside. Additional negotiations and adjustments will be needed to bring the two opposing pieces together. Furthermore, a committee that is not willing to reach consensus, which is not willing to abandon individual agendas in favor of organizational goals, or which is "hijacked" or dominated by vocal members will make staying on target and the ability to meet deadlines very challenging. Committee work takes more time than individual decision making, but the results can certainly be worth the investment in time and energy.

# Budgeting Techniques

We have previously talked about general fund and capital budgets, and the various funds contained within them. These and other budgets are classified by the type of accounting and methodology used to maintain, monitor, and evaluate them. Although public institutions use several budget accounting techniques, most seem to fall into one of five classes: line-item, lump-sum, formula, program, or zero-based.

## Line-Item Budgets

The line-item budget is the most commonly used budgeting method employed in public administration and local government. In this type of budget, services, activities, and expected expenses are placed within a certain category, or line, in the budget. Having a series of accounts, sub-accounts, and sub-sub-accounts makes it somewhat easy to use and monitor. For example, a line item in a typical library budget might be "Library Collections." Within that line item, sub-items would be listed, for example, "adult fiction," "children's nonfiction," and "DVDs." The department then can make individuals accountable to one of the sub-items. Line-item budgets are easy to prepare, can be tied to specific goals and objectives, and can help in monitoring specific spending trends. The ease and usefulness of comparing specific line items from one fiscal year to another have also made this budgeting process popular in the public administration world, particularly with public libraries.

Public administrators can certainly identify problems with using the line-item budget technique. For example, although it might make tying funds to specific department goals easy, it does complicate tying line-item allocations to the missions and objectives of the organization as a whole. Another significant issue with using the line-item technique is the fact that it may perpetuate errors from fiscal year to fiscal year. For instance, I have heard of librarians allocating funds to certain line items simply because the line item is there. No consideration is given from fiscal year to fiscal year as to whether that line item is still necessary.

Some department staff members also complain that line-item budgets become complex and awkward as lines attract sub-lines and sub-lines attract more sub-lines.

With so many lines, do comparisons from fiscal year to fiscal year account for unknown variables? For example, a line item two years ago for library cards may have been bumped up due to a partnership with a school district to increase registration of school children in a one-time push. Year after year, however, the same level of support for library cards is allocated although the registration goal had previously been met.

## Lump-Sum Budgets

The lump-sum budget process should be fairly familiar to students. In this budget process, the department receives one lump sum allocation of funds from the general fund or enterprise fund. The assumption is that the department's managers will reallocate the lump-sum monies into various services and programs to allow the department to operate. The lump-sum method imposes no specific ties to the overall organization's goals and objectives and therefore represents a substantial level of flexibility and internal control at the department level.

## Formula Budgets

Some public institutions employ a mathematic formula to derive the amount of funding that will be allocated to departments. This formula is equally applied to each department and/or unit within the organization. For example, the formula may be tied to the number of staff members in ratio to the number of people in a service area. This budgeting type is more commonly used in academic libraries. However, where public institutions are striving to show that public funds are distributed in a fair and equitable manner, the use of a set numeric formula to determine a dollar amount to be allocated seems quite useful. Unfortunately, this method has a number of weaknesses that are hard to avoid. Notably, formula budgets make it nearly impossible to account for planning, special circumstances, or emergency budget needs. Because most mathematic formulas use variables outside the control of the individual department, formula budgets cannot be considered proactive in meeting community needs. Additionally, the formula used to allocate funds may be using data that we cannot influence or that are not current, making them a challenge to implement in determining and meeting future public demands.

## Program Budgets

Program budgets focus on services provided by the local government. These services are prioritized and weighed against the organization's mission and objectives in determining how much, if any, funding should be allocated to that program. Because of the current push in accountability and responsiveness to the public in public administration, program budgets have become more and more popular. They consider the whole organization's mission and determine how each of the services provided contributes to meeting that mission. If the service is not seen as meeting the organization's mission, then it is either reengineered or eliminated. As you might gather, the city might provide far more services than the budget can support. Prioritizing the services, then, becomes critical to determining which will get funded first.

Cities that involve the citizenry in the public budget cycle often find the program budget technique quite useful because citizens find it far more effective to determine value of a service when it is compared with other services. Similar to a line-item budget, program budgets replace individual-specific items with individual-specific programs. When laid out, this budget technique can certainly facilitate simple comparative analyses among multiple programs. Some public library administrators complain that public safety always wins the biggest part of the budget pie when using this budget technique. When resources are limited, therefore, if you are not in the public safety service, there is little likelihood that all your services and programs will get funded.

## Zero-Based Budgets

Imagine each fiscal year as a blank page on which to construct your budget having little connection to past or current performance. Then suppose you are required to start over and envision what your department's future goals should be. This concept is basically the objective of the zero-based budgeting technique. Starting over from scratch requires the public administrator to prioritize programs in relation to their costs and importance to meeting both the departments' and the whole organization's mission and objectives. Those programs deemed to add enough value to substantiate the costs involved in providing them are prioritized higher. Those that do little to add value are eliminated. We might think of this concept as finding and funding those services and programs that give us the biggest bang for our buck.

One of the advantages of zero-based budgeting is that it does level the playing field and requires all departments, including public safety and libraries, to justify how they add value to the community. It also requires public administrators to develop a cost-to-benefit analysis of providing those services. Does the cost of providing the service exceed the benefits in providing it? Some cities are more likely to fund services such as library services that have a high return on each tax dollar invested in providing the service. Other packages, although perhaps necessary, may be deemed too costly and scrutinized for cost savings.

This focus on identifying programs that will further the organization's future goals and tying them to a cost analysis makes zero-based budgeting popular. The technique is also favored for its focus on effectiveness and efficiency. "Sacred cows" and status quo receive the same scrutiny as all other services and may be identified as unnecessary.

The technique also has drawbacks. Foremost is the amount of time necessary to implement. Starting over each year at zero implies that year after year, each and every aspect of your department's operations will undergo examination and justification. For the most part, library service is rather static, and our services change little from year to year. (That is not to say that the *way* we provide those services does not change.) We tend to evaluate our services on past use and trend analysis, both of which are not considered in the zero-based budgeting technique.

# Public Library Budgets

Because budgeting represents one of the public administrator's most important duties, particularly at the city level, library managers and administrators should anticipate that budgeting at their own department level will be equally critical and expect to devote a high level of attention to it throughout the year. Additionally, communicating budget information and respect for how budget decisions affect the library's service should be continually filtered down the library organization chart. Successfully advocating for limited resources and using those resources in an effective manner will improve the power and authority of any individual in the chain of command. Library managers must learn effective ways to communicate their budget message with upper-level management in the city as well as with the entire library staff. The library manager must realize that the proper "care and feeding" of the department's budget is a crucial element of overall fiscal responsibility in public administration.

How, then, do library administrators impart and distribute this information? How do they show a convincing level of knowledge and understanding of the budget process? The easiest answer to that question is to start with the easiest questions to answer first. For example, you cannot convince anyone that you have grasped the critical nature of the organization's budget if you do not know what the total amount of funding allocated to the library is. You should also understand what percentage of the entire city's budget the library department receives. How does this percentage compare with other departments within the city? What percentage of the library's budget is allocated to personnel? These are only a few of the most critical questions to ask.

Effective library administrators do not put the budget away at the beginning of the new fiscal year, only to wait until the next budget cycle starts. Instead, they realize that the budget cycle requires diligent attention year round. Library administrators must continually monitor the costs allocated and compare these to actual expenditures. Most city finance departments make available a wealth of charts, accounting, and other fund-related statistics to anyone within the organization with the interest in learning what they mean. However, library administrators should not divorce themselves from their own statistical gathering and analysis simply because someone in another department provides data. Our profession has become quite adept at collecting and producing its own statistical reports. Our circulation and acquisition modules within our integrated library system can provide data literally at the push of a few buttons. Therefore, establishing internal systems for monitoring, comparing, and contrasting costs and expenses can and should be used in assisting the administrator to become the only expert on the library department's budget.

Administrators should not overlook opportunities to involve themselves in budgeting processes outside the library. If they feel uncomfortable talking about costs, ratios, accounts receivable, encumbrances, among other issues, it may be a good idea to look into studying accounting or business at a seminar, from a book, or by attending a community college course. A good deal of library administrators have been far more successful at identifying and obtaining outside funding through grants and fundraising simply by showing an increased command of financial accounting and budget knowledge.

## Statistics for Library Administrators

Mentioning statistics to some librarians will likely result in frowns, consternation, and distaste. The library world sometimes views math and statistics with a great deal of reluctance and fear. The only numbers some librarians want to work with are the call numbers on the spines of our books. Still, I'm surprised at the number of library administrators who have access to so much statistical data and either do not know how to collect it or are unwilling to do so. Those public library administrators who do collect and analyze statistical data often do not realize that they are completing fairly sophisticated statistical analysis. Although there is no need to be a statistical genius, it is necessary to gain a fairly complete understanding of why data are collected, the type of statistical data most library administrators find useful in budgeting, and how to calculate simple formulas to present statistical data logically and accurately.

To use and understand statistics, administrators must become comfortable with math. If math is not your forte, do not be discouraged. Luckily, you will need only a few basic formulas. The formulas are easy to compute with a calculator. Also, the data most administrators need to calculate are easy to obtain. Once you have the right pieces and have the correct formula to use, it's simply a matter of doing the math. After having done it several times, you'll find that formulas become easier to use and can often be applied in many situations. You will soon become adept at statistical analysis and be able to show the public, your superiors, and the personnel in the organization that you can account for your library's budget decisions.

## Why Collect Data?

Public library administrators need and use statistics for a wide variety of reasons. In general, regulatory demands, planning, decision making, and problem solving, specifically when dealing with budgeting, are a few reasons. If the library was awarded grants or given other support money, there are often legal obligations to collect data and be able to verify with the funders precisely how the money was used and to what effect. When thinking about the future, administrators will need to be able to use data to project needs as part of the planning process. When faced with a challenge, often there may be several alternative solutions. Using data will be fundamental in helping the administrator choose the best decision. It is hard to argue with factual data. Being able to provide data to substantiate claims or to confirm assumptions helps build trust and acceptance from the organization.

## Types of Data

Basically the public administrator will be dealing with what is known as "quantitative data." These data focus on "how much," "how many," and "how often"—examples of questions that require quantitative data. There is also a need in the public administration world to provide "qualitative data," which answers "how well," "how satisfied," and "why" questions.

The U.S. government's Accounting Standards Board has developed three measurements that most civic organizations, including public libraries, use: input measures, outcome measures (or outputs), and efficiency measures. Input measures are the resources available to the system (such as staff time and funds). Input measures are indicators of the *amount of effort* applied to various services, projects, or programs. Outcomes are those things that the input effort *accomplishes* or produces, such as the cost per person for a program or the staff time/cost required for each unit of service. When public library administrators are asked to measure the efficiency of the library, they most likely try to determine the cost of providing the service to the community.

Many in local government are making a push to measure quality in public government services. Libraries have been slow to catch up. Many of our services are viewed as offering intrinsic value that cannot be calculated. For example, you can show that seventy young children attended a story time, but how does the administrator measure how well the story-time activities promoted reading and learning skills? How do we show that our book discussion groups and computer training courses are contributing to the library's role as a community center? Is there a way to measure direct benefit to activities that are clearly valued by community residents? These are questions that will continue to perplex library administrators unless they can use data to assist them in measuring.

# Common Formulas and Measures for Library Administrators

The formulas and measurements discussed in this section are only a few of the most frequently used and most useful pieces of statistical data a library administrator will need when considering budgets. These formulas are presented only as a representation of the common data the library administrator will calculate. More information on these and other types of statistics can be found on the Web.

### Circulation per Capita

This statistic shows the number of library materials loaned relative to each person in the library service area. The number can be useful in showing the effects of materials expenditures. Has a reduction in your materials budget and your ability to buy more volumes resulted in a reduction of materials loaned? The circulation per capita would be a good place to show this. It can also be useful in showing the library's success in meeting its goal to provide easy access to its services and collections. To calculate this statistic, the library's annual circulation is divided by its service population. If the library's annual circulation is 500,000 and there are 100,000 people living in the library's service area, then the circulation per capita is 5.

### Cost per Capita

This statistic is one of the best methods to convey the library's overall financial support within the city. To calculate this statistic, divide the total operating revenue allocated by the city to the library and divide it by the number of people in the library's service area. When defending library budgets, library administrators will rely on this statistic to show the extent of the local government's financial support for the service (or lack thereof).

### Return on Investment

A number of library studies have attempted to develop a formula for showing the value of the library's service related to the cost of providing that service. Most of these are economic benefit studies that attempt to assign a value to the various services provided by the library in comparison to counterparts in the local marketplace. To calculate this statistic, data from the community attaching a value to each comparable service need to be obtained. For example, what would be the value of the collection to individuals if they were to go out and purchase the materials they borrowed from the local bookstore? What would the cost of using the Internet be if the user went to the local Internet café instead of the library? How much would it cost the family to visit a local movie theater and watch a movie rather than attend a live puppet show at the library? Once you have comparable values for the services you provide, the number is divided by the total amount of tax dollar funding the local government has spent to provide the service to the community. If the local government spent $2 million from the general fund to provide services that are then valued at $5 million, this would represent a benefit of $2.50 for each dollar the local government has invested.

### *Circulation per Staff Member*

One of the best measurements of staff workload is circulation per staff member. This statistic is particularly useful in showing the effects of budget cuts on personnel. A higher number may show that staff members are being more productive. When used in comparison with the same number obtained from other local government, this statistic can show how efficient staff members are in relation to other libraries. The circulation-per-staff-member statistic is obtained by dividing the total annual circulation by the number of full-time equivalent (FTE) positions on your staff. An annual circulation of 500,000 divided by 10 FTE positions would result in a circulation per staff member of 50,000. Some libraries will further filter this number down by finding the 10,000 circulation per staff member (total staff FTE divided by "circulation divided by 10,000") to make the number more manageable.

### *Finding Percentages*

One of the most important calculations and the most useful for administrators is learning to calculate percentages: "What percentage of our community doesn't use the library?" "What is the percentage of library users that are female?" The process of finding percentages is certainly not that difficult. The term "percent," which translates into "for every hundred," is just the clearest way to state how much of every hundred something is. For example, 10 percent of our users are under age eight simply means that for every hundred people who come into your library, ten of them are eight years old or younger. To calculate the percentage, you simply take the amount of something and divide it by the total. Multiply that answer by 100, and you have your percentage: (amount ÷ total) × 100 = percentage.

When dealing with budgets and statistics, one of the most critical functions the library administrator will need to perform is to indicate the percentage something is growing or declining in a particular area. It is also useful when comparing the percent growth or decline of something in two different areas. The easy way to look at calculating this statistic is to think of one number from one time and another number from another time and determine the percentage difference or growth rate between the two. The percent of increase of change (growth rate) from one period to another is calculated as follows. First, determine the change between the two variables by taking the first value (A) and subtracting the second value (B) from it—*do not work with negative numbers*. Next, determine the percent increase (or decline) by dividing that number by the lower number (B). To arrive at the percentage, multiply the result by 100.

For example, this year's budget is $6 million dollars (value A). Last year's budget was $5 million (value B). The difference is $1 million dollars. Divide the difference by the lower number (value B—$5 million) and multiply the result by 100 to get the percentage of 20 percent. Therefore, this year's budget increased by 20 percent from the previous year. The equation would look like this: (A – B) divided by B.

### *Percent Staffing versus Percent Operating Expenses*

The largest expenditure in the general fund's operating budget for most civic departments is for personnel costs (wages and benefits). In many libraries, more than 75 to 80 percent of the entire budget is used to staff the facility. If the figure is extremely high, particularly when compared with other departments and other libraries within the state, this may be an indication that other areas in the library budget have been inadequately funded. For the opposite view, when the percentage is too low, this could be an indication that the library's operations are staffed inappropriately, perhaps the ratio of professional to nonprofessional staff is out of balance. The statistic is calculated by tallying all expenditures for salaries and benefits and dividing that by the sum of all operating expenses.

### *Library Visits per Capita*

Because not everyone who visits the library actually borrows material, it is important to show that people within the community are coming to the library for other services. Showing your funders the number of visits to the library compared with the number of people in your community is a perfect way to do this. This number is calculated by dividing the number of library visitors with the number of people within the entire community. This formula measures the average number of times a person living in the community visits the library. As such, this statistic is an excellent gauge of how well the library's marketing campaign has been in increasing library awareness. Obtaining the number of visitors entering the building should be fairly easy. Many library entrance gates are equipped with automatic counters that track the number of people who enter the building. If not, for the duration of one week, a library volunteer can count library users entering the facility. The legal service area population can be obtained from your city's finance department.

### *Cost to Benefit Analysis*

A common way to find the economic feasibility of something is to do a quick "cost-to-benefit" analysis. Many auditors and public accountants use a much more formal process to evaluate city services; however the process can be done on a smaller scale. A cost-benefit ratio is determined by dividing the actual or projected benefits of a program by the actual or projected costs. The results will often provide an administrator with a clear choice of the best economic option for the department. A wide range of variables, including nonquantitative ones such as quality of life, are considered as part of the calculations. Because the value of so much of what the library provides may be indirect or projected far into the future, it is often hard to quantify in monetary terms, especially benefits from library services such as story times, reading, and programs. However, many libraries are using "present value" of comparable services to ascertain benefits. For example, it might cost $100 to take a family of four out to see a movie. That amount is then used to calculate the benefit of a library program.

## Standards

It is important to note that there are currently no national standards for public library statistics. Public administrators often like to have a benchmark, or set standard, by which they can measure to determine how well (or how poorly) their services stack up. For example, if a national standard were to state that a city should have four to six books per capita as a book collection standard, then a city could compare how its own collection meets that standard. National standards were abandoned by the library profession because public librarians felt that the minimums were being interpreted as the "best possible" and therefore discouraged attempts to excel beyond that. Public librarians also felt that national standards left no room for taking into account the many differences among communities. Instead of measuring our services and budgets by using national standards, library administrators set their own benchmarks, use peer comparisons, or utilize community needs and planning models as benchmarks.

## The Budget Presentation

As discussed earlier, the budget cycle usually consists of opportunities for public library administrators to "present" their budget proposal to various audiences. The budget presentation requires careful consideration and planning to say what needs to be said in a fashion that your audience will understand as well as endorse. Most students of any field have no doubt spent a number of hours watching instructors prattle through a lecture filled with data and formulae. More than likely, the lecture was "assisted" by some sort of presentation tool such as PowerPoint. In today's public administration world, presentations that use a similar form of graphics software along with a computer image projection have become the preferred method of making budget presentations to local government bodies and citizens. With the assumption that "one picture is worth a thousand words," administrators and department heads have become adept at making sophisticated and attractive budget presentations to get their message heard.

Certainly those presentations that make a statement using graphics that tell a story along with sound logic and data to back up their stories have been far more successful than presentations that do not utilize any form of presentation. As was mentioned earlier in our discussion of the budget cycle, all department heads or administrators will be called on to make their budget proposal, so using the best tools at your disposal will be critical. The lesson then is that public administrators should consider their budget proposal as a presentation and should make their presentation soar.

Many classes, workshops, and seminars focus solely on making effective presentations, and administrators should certainly consider investing the time and money into these programs to improve their own skills. In general, however, certain basic design principles are universally acknowledged as prudent presentation "etiquette." First, the presenter should think twice about packing the presentation with quirky sounds, animation, and gaudy text. Use colors that are pleasant rather than garish. A nice blue background onto which white text is placed is far more attractive and easy to read then a yellow background and white text! Concentrate on the one or two key points you want your budget message to convey, and focus on those. Enhancing those points that best promote your message will be far more effective than overloading your presentation with numbers and data that, although meaningful to you, may be lost on your audience. Having talking points that will motivate and encourage your audience to act whether that audience comprises the city council, the city manager, library staff, or citizens should be your goal.

Before making your budget presentations, become comfortable with your budget numbers. Know what they mean and be able to explain or rationalize them succinctly. Make sure your numbers are accurate and that your audience can understand them as well as you do. To understand your numbers, it may be necessary for your audience first to understand the programs you are advocating. You can reiterate the benefits your library provides in the organization's success at meeting its mission and objectives, and the benefits to the community. Public administrators appreciate knowing "return on investment" and "benefit to cost" numbers, so focusing your presentation from that perspective will be extremely useful and increase your effectiveness.

A fine line is drawn between not overwhelming your audience with data and providing enough data to be believable and effective. As a rule, it's better to be able to provide the data orally if called on to do so rather than clouding your visual presentation with numbers. Another effective tactic is to distribute a printed line-item budget detail in advance and provide only the basic details orally in your presentation. Of course a good portion of your presentation will be dictated by the demands and instructions from the city manager regarding administrative presentations, but always be prepared to relate your line-item budget number to the overall benefits of the organization and its mission. Arm yourself with examples of your library programs' effectiveness. Public administrators and elected officials love to see concrete examples of valid "stories" that support statistical claims. If you have performed efficiency reviews and performance audits (discussed later in this book), these are also excellent tools for piecing together budget requests with your presentation.

One final suggestion is to remember the audience to whom you are making the presentation. Remember, they may not know your lingo or professional jargon. Discussing "circulation" or "holds" might mean different things to an audience unfamiliar with library jargon. Perhaps it would be better to discuss "checkouts" and "requests for material" instead. Your audience may have time constraints as well. Nothing can kill an effective presentation more than going on longer than necessary. Say what you need to say, provide your evidence, tie it to the organization's ability to be effective, and conclude. I have rarely seen public library administrators make basic budget presentations longer than 10 to 15 minutes.

Using these and other effective budget presentation guidelines will demonstrate to your entire local government that you, the public library administrator, understand the role the library must play in successfully meeting the organization's mission. It will also show your audience the critical role the public library administrator plays in the whole city structure and the integral role he or she plays in the city's management team.

## Public Money Accountability

The final section of this chapter focuses on the ways public administrators account for the responsibility they have in spending public money wisely to accomplish their goals. Public administrators must provide their community "reasonable assurance" about whether the financial statements of their organization present a real, fair, and accurate picture of the financial status of the local government and the stated results of its spending operations. This is done in the form of an official financial *audit,* which critically analyzes and verifies the accounting statements and principles utilized by the organization. The two most common types of audits an organization can complete are discussed in the next sections. You can find detailed standards and explanations of these and other types of audits at the American Institute of Certified Public Accountants Web site (www.aicpa.org).

### Financial Audit

Financial-related audits are usually performed by an accounting firm that is completely independent from the local government jurisdiction. This ensures that there is no bias because the independent firm would have no interest in concealing or misrepresenting its findings. The independent audit determines several items. First, it will show whether the local government's financial information has been prepared in accordance with established or stated criteria. Second, the audit determines whether the organization has followed specific financial compliance requirements. Finally, the audit confirms that the local government organization's own internal control structure suitably safeguards its assets and has been implemented correctly to achieve desired control objectives. The audit critically examines the city's financial statements, such as revenue and expense reports, cash receipts and disbursements, its assets, budget requests, and variances between estimated and actual financial performance. The successful audit not only provides the community with comfort that the spending of public money is being scrutinized, it also provides the organization with legal protection that verifies financial related laws and regulations have been met.

## Performance Audits

Another type of audit examines the operational efficiency of programs offered by departments throughout the local government. These audits, called "performance audits," provide an independent assessment of the objectives and operation of a program, activity, or function of the local government such as "library service." These audits look for evidence that the program is organized, operating, and performing as effectively and efficiently as possible. Program audits may, for example, evaluate whether objectives of a new or ongoing program are proper, suitable, or relevant. They also can determine the extent to which a program achieves a desired level of program results. Program audits evaluate the effectiveness of the entire program or individual components of the program (or both). It should identify factors that are preventing the program from achieving satisfactory performance, determine whether management has seriously considered alternatives for providing the program more effectively and at a lower cost, and analyze the system for measuring, monitoring, and reporting the program's effectiveness. The performance audit may also provide specific methods, policy, and procedure for improving the operation of the program, thereby improving public accountability.

Performance audits of local government departments, including public libraries, have become more common as public administrators strive to become more efficient at doing more with less. A well-documented performance audit could provide a needed "fresh eye" perspective from an auditor outside the normal operation. An auditor may identify the causes of inefficiencies or uneconomical practices and provide the administrator with a set of alternatives to fix the problem. Another valuable reason for completing a performance audit is to help the public administrator understand the extent to which the department's desired goals and objectives are being met. Most performance audits provide a detailed analysis of the operational effectiveness by spending a good deal of time watching staff members perform activities, questioning them about operations, and looking for input on the value of various functions completed throughout the department. Many library administrators have had success in acquiring the appropriate type, quality, and amount of resources necessary to complete their operations by tying budget proposals to recommendations made by a performance auditor.

With the budget in place, planning can begin. The next chapter introduces the planning processes.

# CHAPTER 6

## Planning

Public library administrators need to know about planning in two capacities. First, there is the citywide plan coordinated through the planning department that directs so much of what the local government growth, development, and future operation will look like. Then there is the basic planning activity that is an integral part of the duties of any manager in developing the strategic direction of his or her unit or department. This chapter investigates both of these facets of planning because a public library administrator will be, in some way, involved in both.

## The City Planning Process

Among the many jobs and responsibilities public administrators and elected officials have is to determine the future look and feel of their community. They must be forward thinking and envision their city's general physical characteristics and how those are likely to change to meet present and future demands. Local government and communities use local planning and their city planners to help them shape their current physical growth and future development. Local planning activities tend to focus on land use ranging from how to develop new vacant pieces of land, to thinking of a new way to use an existing structure, to envisioning larger and more drastic changes of entire neighborhoods. They ask questions such as, "what new buildings and facilities will be necessary to improve public service in this city?" and "where should commercial, residential, and industrial components be placed in this city?" Public library administrators and their personnel can benefit from understanding planning principles. Understanding these principles will help us turn our libraries into vital community places that offer programs, public uses, and customer-friendly public spaces that build local value and serve community needs.

## Why Cities Need to Plan

Abraham Lincoln once said, "The best way to predict your future is to create it." Obviously, the president understood the need for planning to reach one's goals. In much the same fashion, communities and local government need goals and standards that will drive future development in a direction that is appropriate and that makes sense to the overall mission and objectives of the city. Planning helps establish these goals, providing a needed mechanism for creating the future. It should help administrators develop the character of the city. In general, though, city government needs to plan for its future for three main reasons:

### 1. Planning Saves Money

A good plan will help determine the infrastructure the city should have, including considerations such as roads, bridges, highways, public transportation, sewage systems, utilities, and buildings. For many citizens, infrastructure is what determines whether the community is a good or bad place to live. Making the infrastructure work or showing that you are planning for it can attract businesses, taxpayers, and investors. Determining what the infrastructure will be in the future can also save on operational and service costs by promoting efficiency, avoiding duplication, and setting appropriate building sizes.

### 2. Planning Creates a Sense of Community

Most cities have a unique identity—a charm or character that is often tied to the architecture and environmental aesthetic of the community. Planning can ensure that these elements are incorporated into the community projects, buildings, and public facilities. The art of planning also helps to establish a sense of place—the features and characteristics that define the unique identity of the community.

### 3. Planning Protects the Community

Determining how, when, where, and the way places are constructed, renovated, and maintained will affect the community members' behavior and, as a result, their physical and mental health. Plans protect the environment, set aside parks and open spaces restricted from development, and provide citizens with opportunities to improve their health by increasing their ability to access and participate in recreational and physical activity, all the while reducing their exposure to environmental dangers and health hazards. At the same time, home and property values increase when communities plan for parks, playgrounds, transportation, and other amenities.

# Planning Legislation

Before any development of land, services, or facilities in a community, obtaining the "permission" of city planners is definitely required. Cities and towns have created a vast number of laws and ordinances to control the way their communities grow. These laws form the core documents against which planners approve or deny applications for development and building in the city. The city's planners consider how the proposed development impacts the community and verify that they fit within the parameters set forth in existing documents and legislation.

Planners receive applications from developers and residents for projects within the city, and they will guide applicants through the process of getting approval, telling them how and why proposed projects meet legislative guidelines. Projects usually cannot proceed unless the planners have issued permits and development licenses, which ensure that the development meets the local government's legislative requirements.

## The General Plan

The largest and most important planning project a local government jurisdiction can undertake is the creation (or revision) and adoption of a general plan. Sometimes called a comprehensive plan, an urban plan, or a master plan, this document, after it is adopted by the vote of the community and its elected officials, is the community's official statement of policies dictating the way it intends to move forward and physically develop. Some public administrators consider the general plan a "blueprint" for community development. It utilizes the community's values, mission, and objectives in determining future community needs and growth. Just as a home or other building cannot be constructed without architectural blueprints, a city cannot be planned without having a general plan specifying land use, building standards, mission, objectives, and community values to guide its decision-making process.

## A Public Policy

Why is the general plan so critical? The plan is a public policy. As a public policy, it must be approved by the public and enforced by public administrators. The general plan affects everyone and every place within the community. No other public document controls so much about what can and cannot be done in terms of development and land use in a city. When making decisions about quality of life in a community, elected officials and city personnel are, in most cases, legally bound to the policies set forth in their city's general plan.

## The Library and the General Plan

How might the library be affected by the general plan? Suppose the library's service area has grown so large that one facility is no longer adequate to provide services. The general plan should have predicted the need for additional services and provided for future construction of additional library facilities in the community. Furthermore, the general plan will likely have dictated precise areas or locations for expansion of library services. Because the general plan designs the services, types of neighborhoods, and types of businesses that can exist in a city as well as where they can geographically be located, it provides an answer to "why can't the library be located there?" As the community changes, and the need for amending a current general plan becomes inevitable, the public library administrator may be called on to help shape the content of a new amended document. Therefore, bringing the public library perspective, expertise, and vision will have long-range effects on future library service.

# Involving the Public in City Planning

Having as much citizen participation as possible in the planning process is critical to ensure that policy makers have made decisions that incorporate the wants, needs, and demands of the public. Having the public involved also ensures that local knowledge and experience are incorporated into the decision-making process. It ensures fairness and legitimacy by having the public engaged in the planning process. Plans that have incorporated public input will also withstand the need to constantly amend or update them. Finally, having a plan that has been enhanced with public involvement and feedback will reduce some of the potential for ongoing citizen and business disputes taking place before city councils, boards of supervisors, and planning commissions.

# Library Strategic Planning

Now that we have discussed the role of planning in its core role of city operational management, we turn to its more strategic role. Public library administrators avail in a continual planning process to improve library services and envision their library's role in the city's future. At its roots, planning acts as an effective decision-making tool. Public library administrators need to make decisions about what resources services and facilities will need in the short and long term. They need to decide what future library user needs, wants, and demands will be to ensure that their service remains relevant and useful to the community. What resources will be available in the future, and how must those resources be allocated? How might the organization's goals and objectives change, and how can the library situate itself to ensure that goals are met in the most effective and efficient way? Making these sorts of critical decisions requires a sound strategy to deal with issues that may or may not be readily apparent.

Most every business has a plan that lays out its product or service strategy, plans that will help them remain relevant to customers and changing consumer trends. Public library administrators need to utilize the same strategic planning approach that these businesses and retailers use to determine how their marketing, finances, technology, and operational departments will adjust to changing times.

## What Is a Strategic Plan?

A strategic plan is a document that establishes "priorities" for an organization. It should be logical and practical in its attempt to guide your civic program implementation into the future. Because we cannot predict the future, the strategic plan helps us to create the future. The strategic plan projects our desired future and provides a road map to all within the organization the means by which the organization intends to reach its desired goals. The strategic plan must be flexible enough to change when necessary, as well as offer a means by which to evaluate progress toward stated strategic organizational goals.

The library's strategic plan must be developed with of the overall strategic plan of the city in mind. Therefore, knowing what your city's general plan consists of is a crucial preliminary activity to complete before starting your department's own planning activity. While considering the overall city plan, the public library administrator should think about how the library participates, and can continue to participate, in providing for the future needs of the entire organization. A common strategic error results when a library planning process does not take into full account the direction of the parent organization as spelled out in its general plan. This error can certainly affect how successful the library will be in meeting future goals and objectives and in securing the necessary resources to complete them.

### Long Range versus Short-Range Plans

Many public administrators tend to group their planning process into short-range or long-range goals. In essence, the two may be considered part of the same package. Obviously your two sets of goals would not be different. The short-range plan might be thought of as an incremental step used in helping you meet your longer-range plans. The strategic plan is known as a "long-range" plan. It attempts to create a vision of what the library's future will look like ten to twenty years in the future. For most practical purposes, short-range goals focus on the more immediate time frame, from the most current year to perhaps one or two years into the future. Public administrators have a much more solid grasp on what their current situation is and what it is likely to be like next year. Therefore, short-range plans are often easier to prepare. However, the goal of any short- or long-term plan should be to direct your future operations, so continuing to dovetail your short-range plans into the longer-range plan is advisable.

## Parts of the Strategic Plan

Most library strategic plans contain some basic elements that help prepare the organization for the future. These parts include a scan of the environment in which the library exists; identification of the library's mission, vision, and values; the development of the long-range plan; a strategy for implementation; and, finally, the ways and means by which the plan will be evaluated and measured for success. We now examine each of these parts individually and consider how they contribute to the plan itself.

### Environmental Scan

Before public library administrators can concentrate on where they want to go, they have to first understand where they are. Organizations use a process called environmental scanning to delineate and define their professional and physical environment. An environmental scan helps the public library administrator and staff answer the question, "What's currently happening in our environment that has the potential to affect our library's future?" The environmental scan provides the library with answers to "where are we?," "how did we get here?," "where are we going?," and "how will we get there?" questions. The answers to these questions provide the strategic direction the rest of the plan will take. After the environmental scan is completed, the library should have identified the issues and trends that have important implications for our future success as a public organization. The scan will do more than identify these issues and trends, however. It also analyzes and prioritizes them, providing important clues as to the decision making necessary later in the plan. Obviously the environmental scan has some extremely large implications for how successful the strategic plan will be. Therefore, it must take a priority before any other strategic planning should take place.

## Conducting the Environmental Scan

Gathering data is certainly an important step in beginning the environmental scan. This could include community needs assessments, problem statements, and resource allocations data. Essentially, the scan process is asking, "What is happening 'out there' in the library world, and how is it going to affect the library?" To illustrate this point, let's consider an example. Assume you need to go to a job interview across town. Because you cannot be late to your interview, you need to be on time. However, you know that your car is in the shop, so you'll have to take the bus. You do not normally take the bus, so you get on the Internet and research the bus schedules and routes. In doing your research, you identify that the route you need to take is currently undergoing construction and is being rerouted. The alternate route will get you close to where you need to go, but will require you to walk a short distance to the exact address. You decide to allow yourself some extra time to walk the rest of the route. Before stepping out, you also check the local weather and note that rain is in the forecast. You therefore grab your umbrella so that you won't arrive at your interview a soaking mess. The research you have done can be considered a form of environmental scan. You have used your data to make decisions that will affect the rest of your day. An environmental scan for your library will model this simplified example.

Starting with professional research about the library environment from journals, experts, and key stakeholders, among others, and ending with internal sources of data from the library personnel skills, demographics, and labor relations to the usage and collection statistics, you begin the process of gathering necessary data to identify significant trends in its environment and any emerging issues that will likely have strategic implications on your library's future. For example, the process may attempt to identify models and best practices in the library environment, emerging technology, facility issues, and demographic trends. Data-collecting tools are also available to assist the library in collecting environmental data. Surveys, questionnaires, and evaluations are useful tools the library environmental scan can use to collect even more useful data. However, the scan does not stop at merely gathering the data. Careful analysis and interpretation of the data must also take place. This analysis will allow a picture to emerge of the library's internal condition and its external environment and how it has adapted to that environment. It will also provide clues that will help the library evaluate the ways and means of adapting to the emerging trends it has identified.

# The Strategic Framework

Just as a jigsaw puzzle is normally constructed beginning with the outer frame, the library administrator will need to construct an outer frame, a strategic one, from which to build the strategic plan. In this case, the framework consists of the vision, mission, and values for the library. When created effectively and integrated into the day-to-day culture of the library's activities, the vision, mission, and values of your library should act as catalysts to action. They will drive your decision making for the library and should propel your employees to think and act in ways that support and enhance the strategic goals of the organization as a whole.

## 1. The Vision

A vision statement tells the world just what your organization wants to become. It should be constructed with all the members of the library organization in mind and be something that each of them can be proud of, something that every member of the library's community can embrace as their own. A vision should stretch the library to new heights, imagining itself in a superior role or capacity. Most vision statements are short and simple, comprising one or two sentences; some may be just a short phrase or series of words. The shorter the vision statement, the easier it will be for members of your library community (both internally and externally) to remember. The Riverside Public Library in California currently has as its vision, "To be the foremost promoter of self-directed lifelong learning." Community members of Rochester, Maine's public library see themselves as "a model of excellence in library service as perceived by its customers and the library community, with materials, hours, technology, staff and facilities that meet the needs of our changing community." As a part of the strategic plan of the library, the vision statement is a succinct way of taking into account the current status of the library environment and points the direction of where the library wishes to go.

## 2. The Mission

Much has been written in both business and library literature about the need for an organization to have a mission statement. The mission statement, as opposed to the vision statement, is grounded in what you currently do. Whereas the vision statement is a call to action that directs you toward where you see your organization in the future, the mission statement spells out the things you do best right now, every day. Thinking of the two statements in tandem, you might think of your mission statement as the things your library does so well that allows you to envision the future the way you do.

The common belief in business is to think of your organizational mission as describing what business you are in and who your customers are. Certainly these things should be a consideration of your strategic plan. However, developing your mission statement this way does little to help strategically and actively direct your library forward to that place your library visions itself in the future. Therefore, your mission statement should be one of *action* using active verbs, for example, "we provide . . .," "we exist to . . .," or "we contribute to . . . ." One way to incorporate action into your mission statement would be to have it answer the question, "If our library didn't exist in this community, what would *not* happen?" Is there some constructive transformation or change that your library provides that would not be achieved if you did not exist? If the library disappeared, what community benefits would disappear along with it? Like the vision statement, the mission statement should be short and memorable. The mission statement should engage your library's employees and motivate them in the strategic direction you need to go.

## 3. The Values

As a public administrator, it is important to let your citizens know what your core beliefs and principles are as an organization serving the community. The citizens need to know how your library defines what the acceptable standards are that direct the actions and behavior of library personnel. Rather than allow a situational environment in which employees utilize their own individual value systems (which could conflict with your library's strategic plan), defining the values and roles those within the organization are tied to will be a more productive method of ensuring success and unify your library around one set of agreed-on values. Words such as "teamwork," "integrity," "accessibility," and "respect" are commonly used in public library value statements. Because these statements define the precise belief system the library wishes its personnel to employ while meeting its mission and reaching toward its vision, many administrators rely on the staff to create or develop the organization's values and principles.

## The Development of the Strategic Plan

Quite a few methods are available for approaching the actual development of a strategic plan. Rather than recapping and discussing the merits and the drawbacks of each one individually, you are encouraged to use the myriad of literature available in our profession that focuses specifically on the strategic planning process. The intent of this section is to introduce you to the most common methods and to familiarize you with the primary concerns and issues of developing a library strategic plan.

The method you choose to develop your strategic plan will depend greatly on the local government's organizational "culture," your library's size and the complexity of its organizational structure, and the amount of time you have to complete the plan. Generally, the desire would be to choose a process that provides the best data with the least amount of time and energy. Obviously a strategic plan should be given a serious and thorough effort. However, the process should not get bogged down in conflict, hidden tangents, or unnecessary detail.

The first question the library administrator will need to discuss is "who will be involved in the planning process?" For example, will the plan be created internally by library management and staff, or will an outside facilitator be hired to assist in creating the plan? Whichever method is chosen to complete the plan, it seems logical to expect that the library administrator, key personnel and staff, community stakeholders, and community members should have some key role.

## The SWOT Analysis

In generating a strategic set of objectives with their plan, most libraries will complete what is called a SWOT analysis. SWOT is an acronym for Strengths, Weaknesses, Opportunities, and Threats. The organization looks at its internal and external situations (data from the environmental scan becomes critically useful here) and begins to identify the various strengths, weaknesses, opportunities, and threats that will likely have the most impact on its strategic path. Much like the decision-making tool of brainstorming, the goal of the SWOT analysis is to generate a wide list of factors and issues and prioritize them into a manageable set of goals and objectives.

The SWOT analysis first deals with the internal aspects of the library organization, classifying these as strengths and weaknesses. Identifying the many internal factors that affect your organization helps you plan for its future by defining and evaluating how the organization operates right now. These factors may point out trends and failures in your current operations that previously were not known. As stated earlier, the environmental scan data, surveys, and other data may assist in identifying strengths at weaknesses. Likewise, administrators should look at the library's services, its programs, and its funding because these regularly provide perfect internal strengths and weaknesses for your SWOT profile.

Your organization's strengths should describe the positive attributes internal to your organization. These are the things specifically within your control. Ask questions such as "What do we do well?" "What are our best resources?" and "Who are our competitors and how are we better than them?" Your library's strengths are the positive things—perhaps your staff or your amount of community support—setting you apart from others. Your strengths are most likely the things you examined when thinking about your organization's values and principles. Listing as many of your strengths as you can, remind your organization of the benefits you provide to the community.

Next, the SWOT looks at your internal weaknesses. Again, it is important to note that these weaknesses are factors that are still within your control to fix. As an organization that is looking toward its future, noting your weaknesses helps you identify the major issues preventing you from reaching your stated vision. These are the things your grade-school teacher would have marked as "needs improvement" on a report card. In the library world, weaknesses might include things such as lack of a needed skill or expertise, outdated technology, or poor customer service. As you develop the rest of your strategic objectives in the plan your library is developing, your organizational weaknesses are the areas that need attention to ensure your library reaches its strategic goal. Therefore, the more accurately your library identifies its weaknesses, the more productive the SWOT analysis will be.

After the SWOT analysis has looked at the internal factors affecting your organization by looking at those things you have the most control over, you will turn to the external factors. External factors are those that you have little, if any, control over, but that could potentially have a significant impact on your library's future. These are classified as opportunities and threats in your SWOT profile.

Opportunities are those *positive* things within your library environment that represent the potential for your organization to succeed and exceed. Perhaps there is a growing demographic base such as families with children that you've recognized as potential library users. Or perhaps your library is being considered for a large grant for new public Internet computers. Opportunities are situations within someone else's control from which your library stands to benefit. These opportunities may help you plan for expansion or renovation of services. Opportunities may be time-sensitive, and your library needs to be able to act quickly to take advantage of them. Consequently, having a plan in place will be the catalyst to help you capitalize on these opportunities when appropriate and in an appropriate fashion.

The SWOT analysis next looks at external threats to your library. Although threats are indeed external things beyond your library's ability to control, your strategic plan still needs to identify them so that your organization develops alternative plans to address them if or when they occur. Identifying threats means you look for those things that have the potential to have a negative impact on your library. Obviously, public funding availability will be high on the list. A library's ability to offer services will inevitably be tied to the local government budget. When revenue drops—and in the public realm, they surely will—your organization's ability to thrive deteriorates. Existing or potential competition is almost always identified as a threat. A local bookstore opening a block down the street or a competing jurisdiction that has just opened a brand new library will obviously affect your library in a negative way. Journal subscription costs, crime, and so many other threats will likely be identified as part of the SWOT analysis process. Although much on your threats list may be the product of guesswork or speculation, these must still be pointed out. In doing so, the public library administrator will be in a much more advantageous position to identify steps to take now to nullify any potential threat in the future.

# The Action Plan

Armed with pertinent data, a strategic framework, and identification of internal and external factors with the potential to have an impact on the organization in some way, the public library administrator is ready to come up with a course of action, that is, to implement a plan of action that the library will take to reach its strategic vision. The action plan identifies specific goals and objectives related to the strategic vision and mission, assigning a time line and making persons responsible for seeing that the goals and objectives are achieved. Goals and objectives are different pieces of the action plan, and it is necessary to clearly define them. Although goals and objectives both act to move the organization in a certain direction and in a methodical way, the difference between the two can be defined by the level of specificity they express. A goal is stated in more general terms, and applies to a longer term or purpose. It applies to an end zone. A goal addresses a need or an outcome without stating the precise process by which to obtain it. For example, a library goal might be stated, "By the year 2012, the library's use will have increased by 50 percent." As you can see, although there is a time frame and a purpose, there is no indication of how to attain the goal. The attainment factor will be expressed in the form of an objective.

An objective is a specific, measurable outcome that is attainable within a specified time frame. Once achieved, the objective should have led the organization closer to its overall goal. The objective is normally stated in a format that specifies what you will do and when you will do it. It also is stated in a way that allows you to know the point at which you have attained the goal. Using the goal expressed in the earlier example, here are a few measurable objectives that could help lead the library closer to that goal: "By the end of the fiscal year, the library will have purchased 80 percent more best-selling books than it did the previous year" and "The library's youth services team will visit all grade schools in the community in an attempt to get a library card into the hands of every third grader." As you can see, the objectives are more specific; library community members will know if and when the goals have been achieved, helping meet the goal of increasing library use.

# Evaluation and Measurement

With the goals and objectives determined, the time line in place, and specific jobs assigned and specific individuals accountable within the organization, the action plan is implemented and ready to help propel the organization into a new strategic direction. Within the body of the action plan, it is good practice to create a monitoring tool to track the library organization's progress toward its vision. Many organizations make a monthly report to communicate to citizens and staff members whether goals and objectives have been achieved or if they will likely be achieved within the timeframe specified. Sometimes an organization will note that the timeframe specified to complete goals needs to be amended because of unforeseen problems or challenges. Additional funds and equipment might be necessary to achieve goals. Objectives may be revised or new ones added to factor in new information the library has obtained. The library administrator will therefore soon learn that strategic plans need constant attention and commitment to be successful.

Planning is integral to the success of any library administrator. However, no matter how much planning is accomplished, human resources are the heart of any library program.

# CHAPTER 7

## Human Resources and Personnel

All public library administrators want their organizations to be the best they can be. To offer the best service, the organization needs to attract the best employees and focus on how to keep them once they have been placed on the job. The same is true for every department within your city. This is where your local government organization's Human Resources (HR) comes into play. HR (which is sometimes referred to as Personnel) performs much of the administrative work in recruiting and selecting candidates to match job criteria for your library. In addition to these basic services, HR handles activities such as employee training, benefits, and job performance monitoring. This chapter discusses some of the functions handled by city HR departments with which public library administrators need to be familiar.

## The Civil Servant

Most every employee who provides services and skills as a public servant to a local government organization is known as a civil servant. Public administrators employ civil servants to work for their department or agency. It is important to dispel the misconception that civil service jobs are "appointments" that are arbitrarily filled with individuals who cannot be terminated and who will be employed "for life." This misconception comes from ages of popular movies and television programs with civil service characters who were rude tyrants, bound by rules and government bureaucracy and who cared little for the common man.

Although being employed by a local government does offer many benefits, it does not at all mean that employees cannot face discipline or termination. Federal, state, and city civil service codes specifically spell out regulations for continued employment with the local government organization and provide strict testing processes by which employees are evaluated and compensated. These regulations also spell out specifically who can be hired and how they can be disciplined or terminated. Your local government's HR staff can provide you with the civil service code mandating your city's employment process.

## Positions and Classifications

Every employee within the library structure has been hired to fill a position with a carefully constructed job specification plan. These specifications detail the minimum requirements and certain job skills individuals filling a particular position must possess. Individuals who are hired to fill a position must verify by way of their application, resumé, or some sort of examination matrix that they meet the minimum job requirements and possess the job skills needed. Library job classifications are created by the HR department with the assistance of the library staff to ensure that once they are hired, employees possess the skills necessary to do the job successfully. Public library administrators should review their department's job class specifications to ensure they are kept current and reflect new job skill needs. Administrators should ensure that the job specifications they have in place have addressed technology, language, or professional skills that reflect the activities and duties currently taking place within their library and its community.

Every job position within the library organization chart must be funded by the city and department's current budget. If public library administrators decided one day to hire three additional library clerks, they would first need to verify that the additional clerks were funded in the current budget. If the positions were not currently funded, administrators would need to show the city manager and finance director how their departments expected to reallocate current funds to compensate. Consequently, it is rare that new positions are added into a library budget in the middle of a fiscal year—if they are added at all.

Another important note regarding filling positions: it is not a quick process. Because most civil servant positions are bound by civil service rules and regulations that state how long jobs must be posted, how to test, and how to notify candidates, the process can drag on for quite some time. Experience has shown that, in most cases, 120 days or four months will pass from the time the position recruitment begins until the time an employee is placed in your library or unit.

# Recruiting

At some point the inevitable will occur, and someone within the library's organization chart will vacate a position. Employees retire, get promoted, are terminated, move out of the organization, or, in the extreme, die. When a position becomes vacant, the civil service process of appropriately filling that vacancy is implemented. The first question the public administrator needs to ask is "has the position been funded for the fiscal year in the library's budget?" If the position has been budgeted, the process of filling the vacancy can begin. The public library administrator works with the HR department to complete the necessary paperwork. The HR department will check the job classifications to see what skills and abilities are required and then check to see whether there is already a list of qualified candidates who meet the requirements. If such a list does not exist, the position must be posted and potential candidates recruited. Eligible candidates must submit an application and verify that they meet minimum job requirements.

# The Testing Process

How do potential candidates verify that they are qualified to work in the position the library needs? Most local government civil service rules require that the city offer a standard test—written, oral, or both. The test proposes a set of questions that have been developed by HR with the assistance of the library department. These tests (which are most often multiple-choice questions focusing on the specifics of each individual job) are graded, and a list of eligible candidates, ranked from highest to lowest, is created. HR uses this eligibility list to identify the top candidates to invite in for an interview.

# The Eligibility List

Many civil service rules require that lists of candidates who have previously verified that they meet the minimum requirements necessary to fill a particular job—that is, an eligibility list—be kept on file for a certain length of time, normally six months.

These eligibility lists can often be renewed several times at six-month intervals before they become outdated and are thrown away. Having a "qualified candidates" eligibility list available speeds the selection process and reduces expenses to the organization because HR would not have to recruit and retest each and every time the need to fill a position arises.

Although local government municipalities use eligibility lists in slightly different ways, most tend to use a "10 to 1" ratio in filling positions. That is, for every one position that is vacant, the city will interview the top ten candidates on the eligibility list. Some cities also provide "credit" or extra points to employees already working within the organization. These employees bring seniority and experience, and the extra points may place them higher on the eligibility list, thereby improving their likelihood of being called in for an interview.

# Oral Interview Boards

The HR department invites candidates on the eligibility list to complete the rest of the testing process. Normally, the next step involves an oral interview with HR representatives and managers from other jurisdictions who form an "oral board" that will help impartially evaluate candidates. The board devises a list of situational questions to propose to candidates to help them evaluate their skills and abilities. During the course of the interview test, raters use a standard form provided by HR to evaluate each candidate equally using the same criteria. It is important to note that each candidate must be asked the same questions and that there are certain questions such as age, ethnicity, marital status, and religion that cannot be asked of candidates. At the close of the oral board, the raters go over their evaluations of the candidates with one another, discussing pros and cons. The raters then rank candidates from highest to lowest, making a recommendation to the HR representative of who should be scheduled for follow-up interviews.

The follow-up interviews will normally be with the department manager(s) who have the vacant position in their unit and who will be the direct supervisor(s) of the employee. Again, a set of questions is designed and asked of each candidate. The candidates are evaluated by the managers to ascertain who they believe will be the best fit for the department. The name of that person is passed up to the "appointing authority" (usually the department head or city manager), and the hiring process is implemented.

The HR representative will likely sit in on the interview process without being directly involved. During the hiring process, HR will be involved insomuch as it needs to keep a record of the process and ensure that each candidate is considered fairly, that they have each been asked the same questions, and that none of them have been asked an inappropriate question. At the end of the process, the HR representative will collect all the notes and forms completed by the raters, as well as all the questions and other records pertaining to the interviews, and file them.

## The Job Offer

Once a candidate has been chosen, the HR department works to clear the person for employment. The hiring process begins with an offer of employment. The candidate is notified that he or she has been selected. If a salary range is in place, the individual will be told the starting salary. Depending on the job position being filled, the salary may be negotiated. Furthermore, the hiring process may involve a background check of the individual, checking of references, and verifying the individual's employment record. After all preliminary checks are satisfactorily met, the employee is given a start date, and orientation and training begins.

Public library administrators should remember that new employees work for the city first, and then for the library department. The new employee will likely spend their first hours on the job meeting with the HR department. This allows the city to orientate the new employee on matters such as payroll, benefits, holidays, and city-wide policies. The city may also issue identification cards, fingerprint new employees, and take care of other "housekeeping" matters. Another critical "orientation" matter HR will likely discuss with the employee is the "probationary period" and evaluation schedule.

## Probation

All new employees need to understand that although they are indeed on the city payroll, they are still participating in the testing process. This process, called the probationary period, is the length during which employees are trained to perform their assigned duties and asked to show their supervisor that they can perform as they have been taught. During the employees' probation period, which is usually six months for a full-time employee, they are evaluated at intervals along the way as to how well they meet their training goals. As part of the testing process, employees can be told that they have not passed the probationary test, and any employee can be terminated with little if any recourse. Obviously, it is in both the employee's and the city's best interest to terminate an employee who does not seem to be meeting training goals. Although it is important to give employees every opportunity to succeed, spending too much time training, retraining, and working with recurring problems only to terminate the employee just before the end of the probationary period is costly and counterproductive.

At the conclusion of the probationary period, the employee receives a final probationary review from the supervisor, and HR is notified that the employee has satisfactorily completed his or her probationary test. The HR department will then reclassify the employee from probationary to permanent status. Civil service employees who have reached permanent status have far greater protection under civil service legislation.

## Training and Staff Development

Many in local government like to consider employees as the organization's greatest asset, our best resource. In fact, it is from this belief that the HR department derives its name. Seeing our employees as a resource through which our organizations can succeed, the HR department focuses on ways to improve and enhance this critical resource. Much of the focus is placed on teaching and developing employees to undertake a higher level of performance through training programs, education, or professional conferences. Be it "customer service improvement," "interviewing skills," "job safety," "sexual harassment prevention," or other programs, HR departments in the public realm create citywide training with the goal of retaining the employees we have and providing them with the means to improve themselves or their jobs.

At the department level, administrators and their staff must also design methods that systematically attempt to improve employees. At the public library, a new employee will need a substantial amount of training and acclimating to the library and city organizational culture. After providing the "basic overview," training and orientating the employee to the city's policies and processes, most HR departments will leave the effort of job-specific training for the employee to the individual department.

When public libraries do a good deal of hiring and have high staff turnover, it certainly makes sense for the department to create an orientation packet for new employees. Although directors in small public libraries have fewer hires, it is helpful to have an orientation packet, which might include a library card, library department policies, important contact phone numbers, a tour of the building, scheduling information, an organization chart, and specific information regarding the job, such as circulation training manuals or database instruction.

# Library Association Conferences

One of the most important opportunities for staff development in the library world is the library association conference. Library associations are created to promote, advocate, and improve library services in a variety of ways. For example, as part of their mission, many associations have the goal of stimulating the career development of library professionals. This is done primarily through workshops, seminars, presentations, and training events held at professional conferences for library staff. Several national library association annual conferences, particularly the American Library Association and the Public Library Association, should be high on the list of those considered for excellent staff development opportunities that are specifically tailored to the library professional. Additionally, each state has a library association of its own and holds at least one annual conference. Not only do the state library association conferences focus on issues and challenges unique to their individual state, they also are local opportunities for library staff members that may be unable to travel longer distances to attend a national association conference.

# Performance Evaluation

As mentioned earlier, civil servants (employees in public service roles) are protected by certain sets of civil service rules. Cities and local government also receive protection from civil service rules in that they outline a set of standards to which each employee is bound to meet or else be subjected to disciplinary actions. The HR department for each city provides public administrators in each department with this process and performs the administrative role in tracking, filing, and following up on the employee performance and evaluation. This evaluation process allows supervisors to systematically and equitably evaluate each and every employee in the organization, propelling them to lift the organization up in its goal and mission or to improve performance issues before they become a detriment to the same. The evaluation framework designed by HR and used by the city involves 1) target and goal setting, 2) tracking and monitoring performance, 3) rating performance, and 4) rewarding performance.

## Target and Goal Setting

Just as planning is an important part of the organization as a whole, planning also plays an important role in employee performance evaluations. Public administrators are required to implement performance expectations and goals for each job classification. HR will normally provide a copy of these expectations to the new employee, and the employee's supervisor should be well aware of what is expected of individuals in each job classification that they manage.

At the department level, the library director assists employees in understanding their job classification and expectations as they are applied to the library environment. Employees need to understand not only what needs to be done and why but also how they will know if they have done the right things in the right way. Therefore, the director needs to explain the performance "measurement" criteria and translate that for employees working in the library. In addition to these job element expectations, library directors provide more specific targets to which employees are held accountable. The following example may help to illustrate the various levels of job elements or standards to which an employee is likely to be held accountable. HR may provide the element "Performs clerical duties and customer service" for all library clerks, and directors would evaluate each library clerk using that same key job element, among others. However, the job-specific target for each clerk may be different. One may have a target stating, "Shelves 160 books per hour," and another clerk may have a target that says "Inputs data into the circulation system with no more than 4 errors per 100." As you can see, targets should be attainable, measurable, and tied specifically to the job the individual completes.

## Tracking and Monitoring Performance

Tracking performance periods ensures that employees are continually receiving feedback on how well they are meeting targets and job elements. This "check and balance" system ensures that if employees are not meeting predetermined standards, there will still be time for the employee to make changes, and he or she can be coached to improve or adapt. HR departments will normally notify library directors when the time has come to complete an employee performance evaluation. Evaluations are normally tied to the date employees became permanent, and they are most often conducted annually. As stated earlier, probationary periods have more frequent evaluations, and it is important that the supervisor keep ahead of the process because in many city organizations, if the director misses the due date of the evaluation for a probationary period, the employee passes automatically by default.

## Rating Performances

Most local government organizations utilize a standard form on which every employee is evaluated. The job classification's key elements and the employee's job-specific targets are delineated on the standard form, and the director provides appropriate ratings. The HR department will provide guidelines and criteria for assignment ratings. For example, every job element may need to be rated Excellent, Above Standard, Standard, Below Standard, or Needs Improvement. HR would provide the job-element criteria that would presume each level of rating. Employee ratings are based on work that has been performed during a predetermined appraisal period, for example, annually. Along with ratings for each of the key elements of the employee's job, detailed evaluation remarks are provided to help rationalize the ratings received. Ratings are important to employees because they often have an impact on a variety of other personnel actions, such as pay increases.

## Rewarding Performance

Performance evaluations are a formal means to reward employees. The most common form of reward is a salary increase. In most every public position, salary increases are tied to satisfactory completion of the job evaluation. Job classifications each have a salary range with several steps. Each step represents a higher level of salary. After an employee has been evaluated and satisfactorily proven that he or she met or exceeded the standards set for the position, that employee would be moved to the next highest level.

Job evaluation performed on an annual basis often lulls directors into the false notion that they do not have to provide feedback to the employee until the next evaluation. This is not only wrong, it also does not provide incentive for the employee to be more productive and take pride in the job that they do. Such feedback is given in the form of rewards. From a simple "thank you" to monetary rewards, employees deserve to be recognized for work they do that goes above and beyond what is expected of them.

# Employee Relations

In our efforts to maintain productive, efficient, and healthy working relationships between our organizations and our employees, HR designs policies and procedures that public library administrators are bound to implement in their departments. These policies outline the relationship between the employee and the organization and are designed to contribute to positive productivity and improving staff morale, thereby motivating them to perform well and be productive. These policies help the employee and employer understand what benefits are offered, what they are intended to do, and how to go about receiving them. If there is a discrepancy between what the employee and the employer believes the policy states, HR representatives step in to help arbitrate the issue and come to a conclusion. HR also provides employees and employers with advice about how federal, state, and local regulations are utilized within the organization. Finally, establishing positive employee–employer relations means that individuals must be informed that they have certain rights when it comes to appealing or making grievances and what they can do about perceived discriminatory or inequitable practices. This section explores some of the more critical areas within employee relations of which public library administrators should be aware.

## Employee Benefits

In addition to their base salaries, many employees receive a package of incentives or benefits as a result of being employed by the city. These benefits can include vacation leave; holiday pay; health, dental, and life insurance; educational tuition assistance; separation (or severance) pay, and more. These benefits do not come cheaply to the organization. In fact, experience shows that, on average, organizations will spend an additional 40 to 50 cents on benefits for every dollar they spend on payroll.

HR policies addressing how employees will request and receive vacations, how sick leave is to be paid, and how other benefits entitled to employees will be applied must be well understood by the public library administrator. Because these employee benefits are often negotiated with labor groups representing employee groups, they are therefore automatically applied, and the library administrator may have little to say or do about implementing the agreements made between the city and the labor bargaining units. However, not implementing existing policies or implementing them contrary to existing policy will create difficulties for the department and may even result in disciplinary action, fines, or termination.

It is also important to note that not all employees receive benefits. Some "un-benefitted" employees may be working alongside employees who do receive benefits. Additionally, those who do receive benefits may not receive the same type or amounts of benefits as others in the organization. Benefits may be tied to job classifications and levels within the organizational management structure. Many employees see this policy as inequitable, and it can be the root of resentment between the employees and the employer, affecting employee relations in a negative way. However, the public library administrator must not arbitrarily decide which HR policies are good ones and which are bad. When unsure about certain HR policies, the public administrator should work with the HR department representatives and see how to work appropriately through any discrepancies.

## Unions and Labor Organizations

One of the first questions an administrator needs to answer when dealing with employee relations is whether an employee union or labor group exists within the organization. Unions have become important players in the public sector in their role as representative to employees. In the complex working relationship between the employee and the employer, the idea of the "little man" going up against the "corporation" took root in the United States. How can an employee ever hope to gain cooperation and goodwill from a larger and more powerful network of administrators, lawyers, and officials? Added to this distrust, particularly in the private sector, were many incidents of companies taking advantage of employees by working them long hours, providing unsafe and unhealthy working environments, and refusing to compensate individuals equitably.

Federal legislation allowed workers to organize and form cooperative organizations that could represent employees and act in the best interest of the employee. Union members support the activities of the union by paying dues and by electing union leaders. These people are responsible for representing the collective interests of the union's members when they negotiate with the employer on their behalf. Most often, the HR department administrators work closest with labor groups and their representatives in resolving grievances, bargaining, contract negotiations, and policy disputes.

Unions have been successful in the public sector in representing public employees as they bargain to receive employee benefits. In fact, some of the strongest unions are those within the public sector, particularly public safety worker unions. The product of labor negotiations between the union and the city are normally spelled out in a Memorandum of Understanding (MOU). The MOU is often the one written procedural manual available to administrators of the employee relations and policies agreed on between the unions and the city. If for some reason the MOU is not being followed, or there is a perception that the city has not followed the MOU, labor unions can collectively call upon their members to arrange work actions such as strikes to pressure local governments to follow the agreement or to negotiate better employee benefits. Union bargaining has benefitted employee relations by resulting in policy formulation that favorably deals with issues such as lunch breaks, work schedules, and job responsibilities.

It should be noted that not all employees belong to a union. Some organizations have both unionized and nonunionized employees. In these situations, many of the policies and agreements reached between union leaders and employers may also cover nonunionized workers. Additionally, although the major focus of the union is to protect the interests of its membership as a whole, the union will also represent the interests of individual employees by helping to arbitrate disputes and grievances that pertain to wages, working hours, and other similar issues.

# Federal Legislation

Many of the policies and procedures that have been established through the process of collective bargaining, and those that specify organizational rules, are designed, formulated, and implemented by HR. However, there are also major state and federal legislation that provide guidelines that all public administrators must understand completely. The following are only a few examples of federal legislation that mandate certain activities, and HR will expect public library administrators to ensure compliance.

## *Fair Labor Standards Act*

The Fair Labor Standards Act (FLSA) was passed in 1938 and extended certain rights and protections to employees who are paid an hourly wage. These rights and protections include a requirement that these employees receive extra compensation for any hours worked over their regular scheduled time. FLSA also restricted child labor and wages paid to men and women. By capping the maximum number of weekly hours at forty and declaring a minimum hourly wage, the FLSA was designed to put a ceiling over hours and a floor under wages. Title 29, Chapter 8, Section 202 of the United States Code stated that the objective of FLSA was the "elimination of labor conditions detrimental to the maintenance of the minimum standards of living necessary for health, efficiency and well being of workers."

## *Civil Rights Act of 1964*

The preeminent civil rights legislation in the United States, the Civil Rights Act of 1964, was the first to abolish discrimination in the workforce on the basis of religion, sex, color, and race. Otherwise known as the Equal Employment Opportunity Act, the Civil Rights Act makes it illegal for employers to base any employment-related decision on any of these conditions. The success of this Civil Rights Act paved the way for subsequent legislation such as the Age Discrimination in Employment Act of 1967 and the Americans with Disabilities Act of 1990, which focused on protections for American workers.

## *Family Medical Leave Act*

The Family Medical Leave Act (FMLA) was passed in 1993. It requires all public agencies to provide up to 12 weeks of unpaid leave to employees who face personal medical problems, childbirth, or adoption or the need to care for a family member. The act applies to employees who have worked a specific number of hours with the organization and who intend to return to work at the end of their leave. The city or local government organization is required to continue to pay the employee's benefits and to save his or her job provided he or she returns in the specified amount of time. FMLA was designed to assist employees in balancing work and family lives by allowing them to take a reasonable amount of unpaid leave for specific family-related events without the worry of losing their jobs.

## *Occupational Safety and Health Act of 1970*

Obviously there is benefit for both the employee and employer to reduce occupational hazards. The act encouraged *employees* to reduce if not eliminate accidents in the workplace. Additionally, the act requires *employers* to implement health and safety programs. Therefore, this piece of legislation seeks cooperation from both employee and employer to work together to reduce hazard in the work environment. The act principally established the Occupational Safety and Health Administration (OSHA) to oversee workplace conditions and to enforce the employer's duty to "furnish a place of employment which is free from recognized hazards that are causing or are likely to cause death or serious physical harm."

## *Americans with Disabilities Act*

This important piece of legislation extended equal opportunity protection for the first time to persons with a physical disability. The Americans with Disabilities Act (ADA) specifies that an employer must make reasonable effort to accommodate any disabled employee's functional limitations. ADA has quite a few limitations and requirements as to if and when an employer must accommodate an employee. However, in all cases, the employer must work to engage the employee in determining what constitutes "reasonable" accommodation. ADA has redefined the role of disabled employees in the workforce. Today, most employers in the public sector have come to accept the rightful place of disabled individuals within our organizations.

## *Sexual Harassment Prevention Law*

The Equal Employment Opportunity Commission (EEOC), the agency established as a result of the Civil Rights Act of 1964, issued guidelines in 1980 interpreting the Civil Rights Act law to forbid sexual harassment as a form of sex discrimination. Sexual harassment laws forbid any employer from making job decisions that are conditional to sexual favors. Additionally, employers are trusted with the responsibility of ensuring that the working environment is free from unwanted and inappropriate sexual content. The EEOC defined sexual harassment as "unwelcome sexual advances, requests for sexual favors, and other verbal or physical conduct of a sexual nature when that conduct is made either explicitly or implicitly a term or condition of an individual's employment." Sexual harassment charges are fairly typical in the workforce, particularly in the public sector. Consequently, many public administrators have required managers and supervisors at all levels to take state-mandated training classes on identifying and handling sexual harassment claims. The U.S. Supreme Court identifies two basic types of unlawful sexual harassment. The first involves harassment that results in a tangible employment action. This kind of harassment can be committed only by someone who can make employment decisions such as firing, demotion, and promotion that will affect the victimized employee. The second type of sexual harassment is referred to as "hostile environment." This is the type with which public administrators are far more familiar. Unlike the first type of harassment, which only a supervisor can impose, a "hostile environment" results from unwelcome and inappropriate gender-based conduct of supervisors, coworkers, customers, vendors, or anyone else with whom the victimized employee interacts on the job.

## *Drug-Free Workplace Act of 1988*

Many public administrators mistakenly believe that this act allows for all employers to require a drug test. The Drug-Free Workplace Act applies mainly to federal contractors and grantees. The majority of employers are *not* required to drug test. In fact, most state and local governments have statutes that actually limit or prohibit workplace drug testing unless required for specific jobs.

Learning how to hire, train, and treat employees is important in the public library environment. The next chapter helps public librarians learn to communicate with their communities.

# CHAPTER 8

# Communicating in the Public Realm

Jobs of public library administrators are never more complicated than when they strive to communicate. Administrators are tasked with communicating in many directions. They must communicate up and down through the library's organizational chain of command; they must communicate throughout the local government operational chain with department heads and the city management staff; they must communicate with library support groups such as Friends of the Library and the Library Foundation; they must communicate with internal governing groups such as the Library Board of Trustees or Commissioners; they must communicate with elected officials; and they must communicate with the public.

Ensuring that these many groups hear the same message, understand the same library issues and challenges, and trust the library administration's vision is no easy task. Lack or absence of communication is one of the most often-cited problems identified by staff, managers, administrators, and the public when pointing to organizational effectiveness. Therefore, in understanding public library administration, you can benefit from the study of communication models and the barriers to successful communication.

# Communication Model

Unless one talks to oneself and provides oneself an answer, a communication transaction or informational transfer must involve two or more people. This requires a "sender" of a piece of information and an intended "receiver" of that message. Without a piece of information to communicate or some purpose to compose a message, a sender has no reason to communicate. Without an intended receiver, the person sending the message has no foundation from which decisions can be made on how to package the message, what information to include, or even what language or body of symbols to use to convey the message. Successful communication and transfer of information requires effort from both participants in the equation.

Once a sender and a receiver exist, a communication transfer can take place. The sender must first make critical decisions on how to package or encode the message in such a way that the receiver understands what is being communicated. Encoding a message may simply include deciding what language to speak and how to speak it. For example, if a parent is communicating to a young child, the parent may encode the message in terms and tones easy for the child to understand, choosing vocabulary and signals so that both participants will attach the same meaning to the message. If senders are communicating with someone in a different country or from a different culture, they may choose to encode their message without using idioms or slang that may not be understood by the receiver.

After senders have sent their messages, it is no longer theirs to control. They can no longer control how the message is received, what meaning is actually attached to the message, and how the message will be understood. This control rests with the receiver.

The sender's message must be communicated in some format. Messages are sent through channels, and the channel selected by the sender has impact on how and when the message is received. Channels can include face-to-face interaction, telephone conversations, e-mails, letters, digital Web conferencing, and much more. Depending on the message being communicated, some channels are more effective than others. For example, if you are communicating a detailed and long list of instructions, choosing verbal communication as your channel may not be as effective as written instructions. However, in making decisions or seeking feedback, face-to-face meetings offer a channel of communication that is quicker and provides opportunities for clarification and questions.

Receivers of messages attach their own meaning to them; they decode the message. It is important to note that receivers bring their own set of beliefs, feelings, and ideas to the communication exchange. If the sender encoded the message incorrectly by choosing a message that confuses or complicates, the receiver may decode the message incorrectly as well. If the receiver does not take the time to receive the entire message—for example, by not reading the entire e-mail or not following instructions —or if the receiver does not have all the knowledge necessary to decode the sender's message correctly, the message may not be communicated as the sender intended.

Anticipating a successful information transfer between the sender and the receiver, it is unlikely that the communication ends. More often than not, the receiver turns into the sender, encodes a follow-up message, chooses a communication channel, and sends it off to the original sender, who has now become a receiver. This time, the receiver who was the original sender decodes the follow-up message, attaches meaning, and perhaps composes a follow-up message; the two reverse roles over and over again.

# Barriers to Successful Communication

Anything that distracts, distorts, or disturbs the possibility of the sender and receiver sharing the same understanding of a message sent over any channel can be considered a barrier to the act of successful communication. As may be evident from studying the basic communication model, the act of communicating successfully is rife with the potential for problems and misunderstanding. The sender who encodes the message incorrectly or the receiver who does not decode the message properly prevents success in the exchange of information. Furthermore, choosing an inappropriate channel over which to convey a message can damage the potential to communicate successfully. The following sections include common barriers to successful communication: context, environment, background, message length, and emotion. The explanations are intended to assist the reader by identifying situations to avoid while participating as either a sender or a receiver in the information exchange process.

## The Context

Because we and other individuals tend to believe more of what we see with our eyes than what we hear with our ears, the way the sender delivers a message is critical. The sender should pay particular attention to nonverbal cues presented with the verbal message. The body language and hand gestures we choose, the eye contact we make, and the facial features we use all have an impact on the verbal message we convey. Additionally, the tone of our voice, the speed of our speech, and the confidence in the message influence how the receiver will decode a message.

# Environment

Depending on the message conveyed, and particularly in face-to-face situations, the sender should choose an environment conducive to the message. A private message spoken in public or an important message delivered in a noisy and crowded space or in an inadequate environment (too light or too dark) can easily distract the receiver. Anything in the environment in which the communication is taking place that manipulates or changes the proximity between two or more people in a communication transfer, for example, a closed door or high dividers, will likely affect their ability to communicate effectively.

# Background

We all have our own personal and cultural experiences. We have our own beliefs. We have our own biases. Occasionally we bring past organizational experience and organizational culture issues to the communication transfer. These background experiences allow us to use our past to understand something new today. When our experiences change the way we think of things, they can become problematic to the successful exchange of information. Our age, religion, political beliefs, health, race, culture, and gender can each affect the ways we encode and decode our messages. In encoding a message, thought must be taken as to how our background may affect the message as it is decoded on the other end.

# Message Length

Is my message too long for the receiver to comprehend? Have I communicated enough information for the receiver to understand what I need? These are questions the sender of a message must answer carefully. Certainly the content of the message will determine the length, but providing too much information may cause the receiver to "tune out" or paraphrase incorrectly. Providing too little information may cause the receiver to "fill in" with unwanted and unintended information.

Another important aspect in choosing the length of the message must be the communication channel chosen to convey the message. A long message communicated orally over the telephone may get distorted. A short message communicated in writing may have missed critical elements in the sender's mind at the time of encoding and cause confusion and misunderstanding at the receiver's end.

# Emotions

The emotional state of both the sender and receiver affects the successful communication exchange. Barriers are put up when our emotional state (such as anger or fear) distorts the true meaning of our message. A person who is upset may forget important factors in the message. Angry people tend to hear what they want to hear and ignore other pieces of pertinent information in the message. Making ourselves aware of the emotional states of our receiver and what our message could induce allows us to seek ways to mitigate unwanted reactions.

## Active Listening

The average human being speaks at a rate of about 150 words per minute. The average human mind can intelligently absorb more than 600 to 800 words per minute. What does the mind do to fill the gap between what is spoken and what is heard? The listener's and receiver's mind wanders, thinking about other things such as what to eat for lunch or what to prepare for dinner. While listening to the message, the receiver often begins composing a response without completely listening to the entire message. When distracted in this way, the receiver's mind can begin to attach unintended meaning to the sender's message, filling in content that isn't at all implied.

## Improving the Message

In communicating the library's message, the public library administrator should carefully consider the relationship between sender and receiver. "Know your audience" should be the credo in this instance. The message must be constructed with the receiver in mind. Our receiver—the "audience" of our intended message—will provide important clues to how, when, and where to communicate effectively. No matter how careful the administrator is to communicate effectively, it should be understood that there will be many instances when a message has been received in a way that was not intended. Furthermore, a message sent to a receiver may not have been received or received too late. One of the best ways to counteract the likelihood that a message will be lost is to make use of several different channels to communicate the same message. The following list of channels can be effective in dispensing a chosen method.

### *Meetings*

Staff meetings, council meetings, meetings with library support groups or community groups, and meetings with city staff are all excellent forums to spread a message and communicate effectively. An advantage of using meetings as a forum is that the same message can be communicated to large numbers of individuals at the same time. Of course the administrator cannot control how the message is received, but there are far more opportunities for feedback, clarification, and visual cues. Also, communication between sender and receiver is instantaneous. Therefore, using oral communication is often deemed the most appropriate forum for communicating in crisis situations.

Many library administrators find it problematic to hold staff meetings. Staff members are often spread over wide schedules, part-timers work different time shifts, and staffing public desks makes it impossible to get everybody together at the same time to hear the same message. Some library administrators are borrowing ideas from the private world and using "staff huddles" in which staff members are brought together for quick five minute or so rundowns of critical messages, and to share current pertinent information ("Computer number 3 is out of service; we have a music program starting at 4 P.M. today; Jenny is out ill today; we need additional help in the children's picture book area, so everyone please help out and shelve"). For the administrator in a small library, the staff huddle can easily replace a formal staff meeting.

### *Message or Bulletin Boards*

Most work sites have an area where employees are encouraged to check frequently for important work-related messages. Whiteboards or erase boards, chalkboards, or flip charts can be terrific tools for employees and employers. Employers have a central spot to disperse messages. Employees can get into the habit of looking in one spot for department communications. Unfortunately, these formats are "one-way" communication tools. They usually don't provide an opportunity for the receiver to become a sender and participate in the cyclical nature of the communication model. This problem may be aided by electronic bulletin boards or blogs. Many library administrators are exploring intralibrary blogs where staff members can both read and leave messages regarding library matters.

### *Weekly, Monthly, and Annual Reports*

Writing reports is a common daily occurrence of the library administrator's workday. Whether it is communicating to council the reasons a certain piece of equipment is needed or explaining to the library trustees why a policy is being implemented, an administrator constantly puts thoughts to paper to have a written record explaining library operations. Having written communication as a permanent record of the messages sent between two or more individuals allows them to be saved for later study. Obviously, written forms of communication also enable the receiver to take more time in studying and decoding the message and encode any appropriate feedback. A written message does not have to be communicated (sent through a communication channel) immediately. The message can be composed, revised, rewritten, and reorganized over and over before sending. The benefits of editing and revision can be useful in communicating complicated messages or policies. For these reasons, administrators often consider written forms of communication as appropriate for complex business messages, particularly those that include important facts and figures.

### *Electronic Mail (e-mail)*

Electronic mail is perhaps the most popular and most heavily used form of organizational communications. The ability to use e-mail at our desk or from our cell phones to convey important organizational communication quickly and easily, to specific people or to chosen groups, has made it a useful and powerful public administrative the communication tool. To some degree, however, administrators have been using e-mail to the detriment of the communication process. Administrators often forget basic rules of grammar and formatting once used in writing formal letters, reports, or other business correspondence. Administrators who should perhaps consider picking up the phone or seeking other oral communication channels have relied heavily on the ease of e-mail and seek to convey complicated messages using as few characters and sentences as possible. This sloppy correspondence sometimes confuses the receiver, projects an unprofessional attitude, and may ignore the audience of the message. Many administrators have begun to implement strict guidelines on the proper use of e-mail communications within the organization. These guidelines make it clear that all employees are expected to adhere to set standards, that e-mail be used only for business matters, and that e-mail within the business reflects professionalism much as traditional business correspondence does.

## Freedom of Information Act and Public Records Act

Every piece of information created, filed, or recorded by a federal, state, or local government agency is known as a "public record." Because these pieces of communication are public record, many are also public property and must be available and accessible to the public when and if requested. Organizational policies, procedures, meeting minutes, e-mails, and much more are classified as public record. Availability of these records and communication is determined by federal, state, and local regulations. Every state has some form of public records law outlining how citizens must have access to all publicly created records. These laws spell out the process citizens must follow to request public records. Most of these laws have a time frame within which all public record requests must be provided. Often an organization's public records must be provided either free of charge or for a small administrative fee. Public library administrators should become familiar with the particulars of the public records laws within their organizations. The city clerk will often be the best person with whom to talk to find out more about public records requests within your city organization. Essentially, the lesson administrators should take with them regarding public records is that everything you communicate using a communication channel within the public domain is potentially an item that anyone in the public can request and, by law, be provided.

Having hints for communicating with your coworkers and community, you have suggestions for the best ways to make yourself understood. You have also learned that almost any document you create on the job can become open to the public. You are now ready to learn about working with your councils, boards, and commissioners.

# CHAPTER 9

## Councils, Boards, and Commissions

In the previous chapter, public records were discussed, as well as how, legally, most all public records are to be made available to the public for viewing. This is not the only legislation affecting communication and decision making within the public realm. In fact, many local, state, and federal laws will have an impact on the process of conducting business for the public. From the way things are purchased for the organization to the way the decisions are made for citizens and the services we provide them, public laws and legislation spell out specific methods for ensuring the public's interests are served and included. This chapter focuses on the citizen groups that typically interact with and guide the way public library administrators operate. Although much of the discussion covers a "city" situation, a similar structure will be in place if your library falls under the direction of a county board, county commission, or another form of governance. The rules and suggestions that follow serve the library director of the small public library equally well.

## The City Council

The most important, and most powerful, body of local government is the elected officials who sit on the city's council. Arguably, the individuals who are elected to serve on a local council have the potential to directly affect the daily lives of individual community members far more than the individuals we elect on state or national levels. The council of the city in which the library operates ultimately determines how the city's tax dollars and other revenue are spent. For instance, when library administrators need funding to purchase a new integrated library system, to renovate a building, or wants to accept funds awarded from a particular grant, they will likely first need to request approval from the city's council. These decisions and actions must be taken in a public forum.

## Council Meetings

The typical public forum for council activities is the city council meeting. Often these council meetings are held twice a month. Each state has some version of a public meeting law often referred to as a "Sunshine Law" that strictly dictates how these public meetings are to be conducted. For example, there must be an agenda of all action and activity requested from the council at each meeting, and these agendas must be publicly posted several days in advance of the meeting to give citizens enough time to participate if they have questions, comments, or opinions they believe the council must hear before making their decisions.

With few exceptions, public meeting laws state that every part of every meeting of a public agency must be open to public observations and scrutiny. These laws further prohibit council or agency members from discussing actions outside of the public forum. For example, if two or more council members communicated with each other before a public meeting asking one another about how to vote on a particular matter posted on the agenda, this violates public meeting laws because it excludes the public from the process.

Although most cities and agencies handle their public meetings somewhat differently from others, the typical process for the council meeting follows a fairly routine pattern, as described next.

1.  Roll call—The city clerk will call roll to determine which, if any, of the elected officials are present. If any of the officials are absent, there will usually be a call to formally "excuse" the person from the meeting. A certain number of unexcused absences can be grounds for legal action in some jurisdictions. An additional reason for a roll call is to determine whether a "quorum" (usually a majority) of the members exists to allow them to transact public business legally.

2.  Agendas—The agenda is the formal order of business for each council meeting. Depending on the type of local government, the items appearing on the agenda are decided by the mayor, the city manager, or both. Staff and public administrators work with their managers in moving things to the agenda for council action. Once determined, the agenda will be

posted several days in advance and, with few exceptions, items cannot be added to it. At the public meeting, the mayor or council chair will review the agenda that has been posted and ask whether there are any changes or additions. Because of the public meeting laws, items can usually only be added as an emergency and only if the emergency has come up subsequent to the posting of the agenda. More likely than adding something to an agenda, council or staff members are likely to pull something off the agenda. Pulling something off the agenda will usually be the result of staff requiring additional time to analyze and report on an issue, or perhaps the item under consideration is no longer an issue.

3. Reports—Each council member is normally offered time to report to the rest of the council and to the citizens any information and decisions made as part of committees or agencies on which the council member participates. Additionally, if council members have spent public funds attending a conference or training workshop, those council members will usually report to the public what they have learned, any impressions, and other pertinent information of interest to the community in that regard.

4. Work session—The work session is usually an opportunity for the council and staff to work together in jointly identifying preferred methods to handle issues and problems for the community. Often a work session is the process a department head will use to present an issue involving city operations and look for direction from the council in proceeding before bringing official action back to them for approval.

5. Presentations—Each meeting of the city council will likely involve a presentation to a group or an individual in the community who has done something noteworthy for the city or who deserves formal recognition. Usually the city or council member will present a proclamation to the group or individual thanking them for all they do. As an example, during National Library Week, the city's council may wish to congratulate the library for all it does in the community by reading a proclamation and declaring a certain day as the city's "Public Library Day."

6. Official business—The city's legal council will often be asked to report back to the public on any activity or action taken in an official "closed session." Closed sessions may be those involving matters of privacy such as personnel actions or lawsuits that the council is legally allowed to discuss outside of the public forum. However, a report of any action taken must be reported at the public's meeting. Other official business may include approval of previous council meeting minutes, approval payroll warrants, and reports on investments by the city treasurer.

7. Consent Calendar—The Consent calendar contains items submitted by staff or council that are routine in nature. To speed the city's business, all items on the consent calendar will typically be enacted through a single motion by the council unless an item is removed for discussion by a member of the public, staff, or council. A member of the public can comment on items that have been placed on the consent calendar; however, these comments are usually restricted to only three or four minutes.

8. Communications from the public—Each council meeting has a portion during which members of the community can address the council on a matter that is not on the current agenda for that meeting. As a matter of courtesy, members of the public wishing to address the council are usually asked to complete some sort of a "request to speak" form, which is available from the council clerk at the meeting. Once again, public communication to the council at the meetings are normally restricted to a few minutes. Most public meeting laws prohibit a city's council from taking action on or even discussing any items not on the public agenda. Therefore, public communication is usually limited to brief responses by council members to statements made or questions posed. In addition, council members may, on their own initiative or in response to questions posed by the public, ask a question of their own for clarification or provide a reference to staff or other resources for factual information. A council member may request that staff report back to them at a subsequent meeting on a matter brought up by a member of the public. Finally, a member of the city council or the council as a whole may take action to direct staff to place the matter on a future agenda for formal action.

9. City Departments—Most public administrators see the part of a council's meeting that is devoted to city departments as the most important, for it is when matters from individual departments for council action will be presented. For example, a library administrator requesting to purchase a new automated checkout system will likely use the city departments' section as the appropriate time to request action. Before the item is placed on the agenda, the administrator will have worked with the city's manager and provided a staff report relating to the action requested. Each staff report usually provides critical background information, some analysis of the problem, a fiscal impact review, and a recommendation by the public administrator. The report is reviewed and signed by the city manager, and it will usually accompany the agenda distributed to the council. At the meeting, the city manager may ask the department administrator to approach the council to explain the item, answer questions, clarify the staff report, and recommend a preferred action by the council. The mayor or

council may ask for public input or questions, and the matter is then approved or denied by the council.

10. Adjournment—Each council meeting must be officially closed. Matters of the city are then suspended until a predetermined future date as announced on the public agenda. Public administrators then begin preparations for the next meeting, selecting items for consideration to present to the council at its next meeting.

# Commissions and Boards

Cities often provide for citizen participation in city operations by appointing boards or commissions. In fact, many states will actually require cities to form commissions or boards to make certain decisions affecting its citizenry. Planning committees, public safety commissions, and library boards are all examples of the means through which local governments give citizens a voice in their government and provide them with a way to influence decisions that shape the quality of life for the residents of the city. Participation on a board or commission is one of the most effective steps citizens can take to become an active voice in their government.

Board members and commissioners are volunteers appointed by city council members to study community issues, give city staff direction on operational matters, obtain public comment on key projects, and take action or offer recommendations to the council on any number of matters. A notice of an opening for a commission and board often appears in local newspapers, is distributed to community organizations, and is posted in public buildings. Interested applicants submit an application to the city clerk, and council members conduct interviews to select a candidate to serve on the citizen committee.

Most boards and commissions have few requirements other than residency within the city to participate on a particular board. Terms of service vary, but typically fall within two- to three-year increments. Additionally, although citizens volunteer to serve on boards and commissions, some cities do offer a small stipend to members in exchange for their service.

## The Major Functions of Boards and Commissions

Most cities and local government agencies utilize boards and commissions as part of their push to give citizens a voice in the decision-making process. In general, these boards and commissions have five major functions:

1. Administering policy—Boards and commissions of public agencies set policies that have an impact on all operational areas of the organization. They then ensure that the organization operates according to the policies they have set.

2. Finance oversight and control—Boards approve the operational budget and monitor all financial transactions that relate to that budget. The board is responsible for understanding revenue and income expectations as well as being aware of expense allocations. This means that board members need to understand completely where the money the organization spends comes from and agree as to where that money goes.

3. Public and community relations—The board members interpret the work of the organization and translate it for the community. They act as the bridge between the department or agency and its community, opening its doors for the success of the whole enterprise.

4. Program—The board members become familiar with each of the programs and services provided by the organization. They monitor and evaluate the success of these services and ensure that these services move the organization toward its adopted goals.

5. Personnel—A less common role of the board, particularly in the public library world, is to hire and evaluate senior executives. The board also approves personnel policies as they affect the number of employees, job descriptions, and disciplinary policies.

## Staff and Boards

A good deal of confusion exists in the public sector over the relationship between staff and boards. What do boards do, and what should staff do? What is the proper way these two key players in public administration should interact? Here, then, are the important things that distinguish an administrator's role from that of the board member:

1. Recommend polices—The administrator or executive staff recommends policy and policy changes to the board. Because "staff" should be considered the expert in the interaction, and board members administer policy, staff should act as expert advisors to boards and commissions in advancing appropriate policies for the board to consider.

2.  Implement policy—After the policy is adopted by the board, the final form becomes operational through the actions of staff.

3.  Manage operations and services—The administrator and his or her staff operate the services offered using the parameters of the policy set by the board. Budget constraints also affect the management of these services. The board monitors these programs and services and communicates needed policy changes to the administrator for potential board action.

4.  Act as contact for the community—Although board members should be considered ambassadors from the library to the community, the administrator is far more likely to be consulted by the community than any member on the board would be. Therefore, the administrator should act as the eyes, ears, and voice of the board, communicating the need for actions on policies. The face of the organization is sketched and communicated daily by the actions, competency, and demeanor of the administrator and his or her staff.

# Library Boards

Although there are many important boards and commissions that provide important services to the local government, the one of most importance to the public library administrator is that which services the city's library. The Library Board of Trustees, sometimes called the Library Commission, operates much like every other public committee in that its meetings are public, all of its communication is public, and its members serve the interest of the public. Library board members normally number five to seven persons, each appointed by the city council. Library boards are often established as a requirement by state laws or city charters. In California, for example, the state's Education Code (Section 18910) stipulates that public libraries are required to have a governing board. Term limits, procedural matters, membership requirements, board roles, and basic governance may also be established in these codes.

## The Role of the Library Board

The role of the library board differs from jurisdiction to jurisdiction. Some may be classified as "advisory," whereas others are classified as "administrative." Advisory library commissions may analyze and study a specific issue, such as changing the fee structure for the library. They may also provide oversight of a specific library function, such as outreach to the community. However, in either case, the city council remains the decision-making authority for the city. The library board passes on important advisory information to the city council, but it is the council that retains the right to decide any outcome. Many other library boards retain complete administrative control over the decisions and expenditures in regard to the library totally independent of the city council. For example, some library boards are empowered to hire and fire the library director. Whether advisory or administrative, both are empowered to create and approve library policies that specifically pertain to library programs and operations. Many library boards are required to approve, if not altogether prepare, the library's budget.

Regardless of the specific duties, every library board member is expected to be an advocate for the library in the community. They are expected to communicate issues and information continually about the library with the council, working as ambassadors for library services at the local, state, and federal levels of government. All public library administrators must carefully review the legal guideline that establishes the library's board in their city, ascertain which specific library roles the board holds, and determine how to best facilitate those roles.

## Maximizing the Library Board and Director Relationship

Hundreds of articles have been written about the critical, sometimes fragile, relationship between the library director and the library board. A dysfunctional library board can derail productivity and focus and have an impact on the library's strategic direction. A library director who does not respect board members and does not seek their input and feedback will find that each decision becomes a struggle and often results in lack of trust. In an environment where the library board has administrative control, particularly one that has the responsibility to select a library director, a poor relationship between board and director may result in the termination of the administrator's employment. Therefore, there are pragmatic benefits for doing whatever is possible to strengthen the potential for strong, healthy teamwork between board and director. Experience has shown that the following common tips have proven successful in doing just that.

1. **Provide orientation programs for all new board members.** New board members appreciate meeting and getting to know library staff members and fellow board members. A "mixer" or small party may be an excellent way to facilitate this. New board members also need to know the driving factors behind library operations such as the library's mission statement, vision, strategic plan, budget, and facility issues. A library board manual with this key information along with the appropriate legislative codes pertinent to the establishment of the board and the library, its by-laws and the board role and responsibilities in regard to governance,

advocacy, and others is a terrific way to acquaint new trustees or commissioners with information they can pore over now and in the future.

2. **Make board meetings meaningful and productive.** Nothing is more disheartening to board members than requiring them to attend a meeting with no purpose or direction. Include the library board chairman and board members in choosing agenda topics. Agenda topics should be tied to a needed action, such as approval of a policy or providing direction to staff to proceed in one way or another. If an item on the agenda is "informational only," consider the best possible method to convey that information. Each individual on the board should know the process to follow in conducting the meeting in line with existing laws. Staff should ensure that each board member has an agenda and packet of pertinent information at least a week in advance of the meeting. Ensure that meeting minutes are recorded and that the time keeper apprises all members of agenda progress. Finally, ensure that meetings follow existing parliamentary procedures and rules. A refresher session on Roberts Rules of Order may be necessary.

3. **Include library board members in "staff development" programs.** Library conferences, workshops, and local library district meetings provide staff with excellent opportunities to network and learn more about their profession. The same opportunities must be passed on to board members. Part of the role of the library board member is to act as an ambassador for the library, so we must remember to provide them with incentive and ample opportunities to participate. Many library directors plan annual library board retreats that include team-building activities and training. Many times, an outside consultant can help facilitate retreats, bringing an outside, fresh perspective.

4. **Encourage library board members to reach outside the library.** Much of what we do in the library world was "borrowed" from other environments—for example, we borrowed barcode technology from retail and grocery stores. We like to model "best practices" and borrow success stories from other libraries. As community partners, our board members should be encouraged to visit other professional environments and libraries and bring back their experiences participating as a "library user." The board members should feel comfortable in discussing with the library director what people are saying about the library out in the community. If library board members are fielding complaints from community members about things the library should improve, the director and the board member should work as a team to identify ways to make it better and improve library services.

5.  **Talk openly about the relationship between library personnel and the board.** It is useful to include an organization chart in any orientation material provided to new members and to outline the chain of command. Although board members should always feel welcome to thank staff and recognize service, when it comes to discussing library issues, programs, processes, and procedures it must be agreed that these should be brought up only with the library director. It must be expressly understood that the library director has been hired to lead the staff. Staff members should always take their direction from the director or their immediate supervisor. Board members should not request favors or special services from staff members. A board member who requires anything outside the realm of basic library service should ask assistance from the library director rather than from a staff member. For example, a board member who would like to review certain collection statistics should request these from the library director rather than, say, the circulation manager.

6.  **Focus on creating positive relationships between all departments.** In stressful situations, it is occasionally easy for library board members to criticize unpopular decisions made by the council. For example, if the city is experiencing tough economic times and departments are forced to compete against one another for a bigger piece of the budget pie, a council decision that the police and fire departments take smaller cuts than the library department can infuriate board members. Talking about the "big picture" and focusing board members on offering constructive criticism will be an important aspect in keeping the library board from angering council members and jeopardizing a fragile relationship.

## Symptoms of Dysfunctional Board–Staff Relations

As mentioned earlier, the professional literature of many public agencies is filled with case studies in which boards or commissions and staff frustrate the citizen participatory process in dysfunctional roles and behaviors. Although it is beyond the scope of this book to recommend actions to correct dysfunctional relationships, it is advantageous to be able to recognize some dysfunctional symptoms if and when they occur. By recognizing the symptoms of dysfunctional relationships, administrators can quickly seek to obtain more professional assistance in resolving them.

Board members who micromanage each decision made by the library director are overstepping their responsibilities. Suggesting that the color of the wall of the library should be blue is acceptable, but for a board member to bring in a can of blue paint and tell a staff member to paint the wall is inappropriate. A good way to think of board management is to maintain a "gavel to gavel" system. When the board chairman calls a board meeting to order, the board is in charge. When the chair adjourns the meeting, individual board members resume their role as community advocates volunteering their energy and enthusiasm but leaving executive staff in charge to make decisions.

On the flip side, a library director who seeks to hide information or who excludes the board from the decision-making process is circumventing citizen participation in government. Staff must not redirect or implement any program or policy without seeking board permission. Library directors have no authority to change board policy. They must recognize and accept that. Although most organizations honor creativity and innovation, implementation must first have board approval.

Refusing to evaluate ourselves and our services and to listen to the feedback we receive is as detrimental to our organization as it is to our relationship with the board. Staff, customers, and board members all need to know how things are going within the organization and how successfully each is performing in their individual roles. We each hope that the procedures we have enacted and implemented are doing precisely what they were meant to do. As such, we establish procedures that formalize the monitoring, evaluation, and discussion of job and organizational performance. We establish periodic reviews of our success and progress (or lack thereof) toward meeting organizational goals and objectives. If we refuse to build in feedback mechanisms or refuse to abide by those we already have, we will have contributed to the potential for much of the dysfunction that follows.

The old adage that "too many cooks spoil the broth" holds true in board and staff relationships. It must be made completely clear that the public administrator (whether the library director, fire chief, or otherwise) is in charge of the department staff. Board members are in charge, if only theoretically, of the public administrator. Board members who have a need from the organization, or would like to make a "suggestion" for the organization, should funnel their requests through the public administrator in charge of the staff. If board members start giving commands directly to individual staff members, they have usurped the authority of the public administrator, redirected established priorities, jeopardized organizational progress toward goals, and perhaps even destroyed morale. The "gavel to gavel" management style should be in effect, and board members should give direction to the public administrator, holding her or him accountable for organizational goals.

Each board has elected "officers"—the president, vice president, secretary, treasurer, and perhaps others. Officers have terms for a reason. It is never good policy to let one officer stay in place for more than two terms. The board should be generating leaders who are trained to take committee assignments and duties as part of their board responsibilities. Your organization is made up of a team. It is not the realization of any one person's or small group's dream or efforts. Therefore, officers who stagnate in one position limit the board's ability to grow, innovate, and generate new ideas.

To act on a policy decision or other action affecting the organization, any board needs to have a quorum. Boards that do not can simply pass along information without any ability to act on agenda items. Boards that cannot make a quorum frequently cancel meetings without ever having accomplished anything. Boards are a problem for the organization when they often fail to reach quorums, they meet infrequently, or are filled with individuals who wish to leave meetings early because, ostensibly, all activity is blocked. If members cannot make meetings or stay long enough to get business completed, they should be replaced with individuals who are committed to doing the job right.

The governance structure of your library provides the framework for effective services. Working in teams, covered in the next chapter, is also an important part of meeting the needs of the community.

# CHAPTER 10

## Working in Teams

Public administrators work in many team settings. Arguably, they work on many more teams than individuals in other work environments. They work on the executive team with all department heads who strive to solve city-related problems together. They work with boards and commissions in dealing with department-related issues. When the library is large enough, they work with their own department staff teams to move the organization toward its strategic goals. The need to work together and use teams seems especially relevant in local government settings where the popular notion that "two heads are better than one" drives administrators to solve problems by bringing together as many people as possible to address public operations.

Citizens value decisions made by the group rather than the individual. This is why, for instance, we use trial juries to make decisions in court. Our natural inclination is to distrust a decision which has been made without including many different views or without considering alternatives brought to the table for discussion. This chapter discusses teams and teamwork in general, offering common advantages, drawbacks, and pitfalls that public administrators should be keenly aware of.

# What Is a Team?

It is a common myth to think that whenever you bring a group of people together to work on a project, they are instantly a "team." Instead, in such instances, you have only created a group. To have an effective team, the group of people needs to have a common goal. The group members need to agree among themselves that this is the goal toward which they all will strive. Of course, there is a fine line that distinguishes between a group and a team, and it is one that can cause some confusion. Finding a group of people is fairly easy. Suppose you walked into a library and grouped individuals according to height or age. Or perhaps you grouped individuals together relating to their expertise: library clerks here, librarians there, library pages here, and so on. Although the groups share common attributes, they do not bring the same level of effectiveness to the group. The expertise and interpersonal skills of group members could vary extensively.

In contrast, a team has members selected for the complementary skills each brings to a common purpose. A library team may consist of a library clerk, a librarian, and a paraprofessional who have been selected to improve services to young adults at their branch library. Each member of the team has a purpose and a function within that team, and the team's overall success will greatly depend on how well they work together to achieve their specific goal. To illustrate, employees working together in the circulation services unit are a group. They work together to check out and check in material. When members of this group are selected to work on, say, the best ways to increase checkout speed and improve access to the collection, they suddenly become a team. The addition of the specific goal and the individual skills each brings to their collective efforts have elevated them to work as a team. Public administrators should use working in teams to improve their organizations. They should focus on identifying ways to move from group work to team work.

# Building Teams

Building teams that work effectively together is a daunting task, rife with potential for conflict and dysfunction. Many administrators abandon the hard work of building effective teams simply because they do not know how to identify common stages in team building and facilitate the best ways to propel the group toward its goal. On the basis of my years of experience observing and working with teams as well as my experiences teaching management basics to library students, I have learned that a team progresses through a definite pattern of teamwork. Each level adds an important dynamic to the team's interpersonal effectiveness, and each level must be cultivated by the leader to allow the team to move forward. The levels of team building commonly include the following:

1. The formulation stage—During this stage, members are brought together to work on a specific goal. They may be confused particularly on what that goal is and why reaching the goal is necessary. Members perhaps do not know each other or understand the skills they each have brought to the team. Furthermore, members are exploring the boundaries of the group, ascertaining appropriate behavior within the group. Consequently, during this stage of team building, a good deal of the team's time is spent "off task." The team leader should focus on means to cultivate group exchanges and socializing. Ice breakers, orientations, and group interaction exercises are excellent ways to bring team members together and begin to learn more about each other and establish some ground rules and team expectations. A common pitfall in team building is to ignore this stage or spend too little time in allowing group members to interact and exchange information about working on the team.

2. The conflict stage—This stage is sometimes called the "storming stage," and for good reason. Once team members become comfortable with one another, they will begin to focus on the team's task, likely realizing that the task is far more difficult than they originally imagined. Because of this, members fall back to their "comfort zones," putting up defense mechanisms and offering much resistance to the task at hand. In larger teams, cliques begin to form, and resentment and frustration manifest in arguments. During this stage, communication is often poor, and members refuse to listen. Finding effective ways to communicate and to allow the team a mechanism in which to vent frustration are important steps the team leader should take. The leader who embraces conflict during this stage recognizes that the group is in this important stage and expresses confidence in the members' individual skills and abilities in reaching the team's goal. An excellent step at this stage is for the leader to negotiate team roles and responsibilities, always keeping in mind the specific skills team members can bring to these roles.

3. The order stage—A team leader who has successfully moved the team through its formation stage and through the storming and conflict stage will note that the members have more readily accepted the team's purpose, its ground rules, and its roles. The team's added feeling of camaraderie has allowed the team to complete certain tasks moving it toward its goal. This, in turn, has led to even more cooperation between team members. Team members will have a stronger willingness to solve problems.

The team's energy in this stage is at its highest. The team leader can culti-vate this stage by planning and paying attention to detail, never losing sight of the means through which the team supports its own members. The leader must continue to find ways to enhance the team's shared vi-sion. Whether by addressing conflict constructively as a group or by re-inforcing positive group norms, the team leader invites input from the group and enhances team responsibility toward meeting its goal.

4.  The performing stage—We think about this level as the point at which the team has become a finely tuned machine. The team has gained insight into both personal and team processes. As the leader uses individual member talents constructively, the team continues to meet benchmarks and milestones. The cooperation and cohesion between team members is extremely strong because any weaknesses or strengths are recognized and repaired or used appropriately.

5.  Celebrate team successes—Once the team has met its goal, it is important for the group to celebrate its achievement. Celebrating success not only recognizes team members for the work that they have done, it also proves the value of teamwork to the organization, encouraging others to contrib-ute to their own teams in an effective manner.

## Team Size

Little agreement can be found as to "the best" number of employees to assign to a team. The most accurate answer seems to be that the best number of people on a team should be driven by its task and the skills necessary for the team to succeed. Although there may be no hard-and-fast rules or standards to help administrators determine the optimal number of people to assign to a team, there are some considerations that will help determine the likelihood that team size would enhance or hamper the potential for the team to be successful.

The administrator should answer the question, "What type of task or goal will the team complete?" Knowing the answer to this question will help the administrator de-termine who within the organization has the best skills and abilities to offer in com-pleting that goal in the quickest amount of time. If the task absolutely requires many skills and abilities, and individual members have one or two of the skills but not all of them, then the administrator will, out of necessity, be forced to include more people on the team. Additionally, the administrator will need to determine what sort of inter-dependency and coordination between team members will be required to finish the task effectively. A task with an extremely high level of interdependence will require the administrator to look to reduce group size, and therefore the potential for conflict and incongruent dynamics, and focus on selecting team members who are the most likely to "get along."

As a rule, smaller groups, between three and ten people, tend to be more informal and need less guidance. They rely less heavily on rules and roles, and group interaction tends to be higher as more group members feel comfortable in participating in discussions. There tends to be less conflict in small group sizes, and the decisions made by small groups tend to have a higher level of consensus. However, smaller groups do not have the wider depth of input and expertise. A small group dominated by one or two individuals may cause others to be reluctant to contribute to the whole discussion. Consequently, small group decisions may not have been as thoroughly discussed as could be.

A large group, ten or more, certainly increases the number of skills, abilities, and ideas brought to the table. Decisions made by larger teams have a greater potential for acceptance within the organization. However, with larger groups come more potential for conflict. There tends to be less cohesion in larger-sized teams. Cliques form and factions splinter off, sometimes sabotaging group decisions. Larger teams are more complex and will require more formal operations; roles such as secretary and timekeeper will be necessary to ensure that the group does not lose focus. Larger teams need strong leadership to move the members appropriately through the various team-building stages identified earlier in this chapter.

## Team Roles

Whatever the size of the group, the need for members to feel like they belong and have a purpose within the team is an important facet of successful team building. Many roles attributed to group members are well known. Obviously the group leader is an important and necessary role on each team. The team leader helps members through team-building stages and keeps the team focused on its task. Teams also utilize several other traditional "task-oriented" roles. Many need a secretary or note taker, whose job it is to record what is said, who said it, how it was received, and what action was taken. Having a recorded history of the team's interaction is helpful in keeping the group on task and apprised of its progress and accomplishments. Many teams utilize a time keeper who ensures that meetings do not go beyond the agreed-on time limit.

Other roles include, but are certainly not limited to, technicians, team members, and facilitators. Still other team roles have evolved that revolve around the socioemotional aspect of the team's behavior. These individuals ensure that everyone has been included in the discussion. They ask for alternatives. They facilitate resolution of conflict. These less traditional team roles focus on nurturing team members and supporting the group's emotional health. Basically, someone on the team will always need to ensure that an agenda is created, that a room is booked, or that supplies such as flip charts and computers are available for team use. Selecting these individuals for their specific skills in role taking will be a critical part of team-building success.

# Norms

Every team has generally agreed-on informal rules that guide team member behavior. These established rules of behavior or standards of conduct are what are normally referred to as group norms. Norms are useful for teams because they increase the order and predictability of team activity. It must be noted that norms are rarely written rules. They have often been internalized in the group's behavior through a process of socialization and team interaction. Although there are some formal disciplinary consequences to nonconformance to norms, far more likely are the informal consequences in which members are made to feel guilt or shame when team norms are violated.

Norms have different ways of developing. One way a norm can develop is by a set precedent that has taken root over a long period of time—the "that's the way we've always done it" mentality. For example, if the chairman of the team always sits in one specific chair, it would be deemed inappropriate for another member to sit in that spot before the chairman arrives. Another popular trend in developing a norm is by carryover from other environments. If a popular Web resource is deemed by our profession as unauthoritative for use by students in writing a research paper, it will also be considered as inappropriate to use as a resource for the team's research. Finally, a norm may develop out of a critical event in the team's history. If, for example, the team suffered a setback due to one member divulging a piece of information, a norm maintaining confidentiality may arise in team activity.

Norms can be classified into prescriptive and proscriptive categories. The prescriptive norms are expectations by the team of behavior that is supposed to be done. For example, the expectation that every member of the team bring a calendar to the meeting so that future meeting dates can be planned can be classified as a prescriptive norm. The opposite to prescriptive norms are proscriptive one. These are expectations within the team regarding behaviors in which members are not supposed to engage. "We will not text on our cell phones during a meeting" would be an example of a proscriptive norm. Because team norms are often not formally spelled out, learning about them, perhaps during the forming stages of team development before they are inadvertently violated, is a critical area of team building success.

## Developing Successful Teams

Because working in teams is expected in public service and so heavily used by public administrators, it is often surprising that little is done within the organization to ensure that teams function well. It has become far too common for the administrator to select team members for a project and then step back wondering later on why the team could not function effectively. What can public administrators do to optimize the potential for effective and successful use of teams within our organization? The first thing should be to provide training at all levels within the organization in team-building skills. Supporting your organization's teams and teaching employees how to function within teams should be a high priority in public service. Training identifies for your department's teams the pitfalls and problems they will likely face and provides them with the methods to solve them once they do.

Public administrators must give heavy consideration to the tasks they expect teams to handle, selecting the best team members for that task based on the proven skills and abilities each team member has the potential to bring. The administrator must be an effective communicator and impart to the team the specifics and the urgency of the team's mission. The administrator must outline for the team the need and level for cooperation within and between teams. The administrator must offer support (in resources and in organizational will) to the team's decision, recognizing the time it will take to make that decision. Ultimately, the administrator must be patient and give the team time to move between stages of development as it strives to meet its goal.

This chapter has covered building working teams. The next chapter considers problem solving and decision making.

# CHAPTER 11

# Solving Problems and Making Decisions

Whether it is deciding which doctor to take our children to, what route to take to the library, or even what movie to see this weekend, decision making is an activity we all complete on a daily basis. Although we do it continually, few of us would admit to enjoying the decision-making process. It is often time-consuming, costs money, or has risks with which we are not comfortable. Making decisions for the public, what services to offer, what technology to use, or what problems to handle first poses the same feelings of anxiety and frustration for public administrators. Making decisions that involve the good of the public will involve a complex level of decision-making skills, and therefore public administrators must learn to make decisions involving public service in an efficient and effective manner. This chapter explores several problem-solving and decision-making tools that public administrators have at their disposal and that will assist them in making decisions with the greatest chance of being successful once they are implemented.

## The Problem Space

The most frequently encountered problems in the public service realm are those dealing with hiring, facilities, regulations, technology, inventory, training, politics, and emergencies. Problems within these areas usually boil down to the department being in one "state" and needing to be at another. The difference detected between the current state and the desired state is what is often defined as the *problem space*. How do we move from the current state to our desired goal? We choose "operators" that will make the most important difference in helping us eliminate the distance between our current and goal states. An analogy to help illustrate the problem space model is to envision the activity of completing a maze. We ascertain our current position. We then identify where we need to be. Finally, we choose routes that progress in various directions toward our goal. At the exit of the maze in moving toward that goal, we use various operators, such as left turn, right turn, turn around, go back—each designed to move us toward an end state.

In handling routine problems, the operators needed to solve the problem are easily recognized. In trying to determine how much money we need to purchase three items, the operators we choose would be the use of simple addition. Unfortunately, public administrators are most often faced with a problem space that is ill conceived or complex. The operators to choose and the decisions to make in solving the problem are far from evident. For example, the problem, "what is the best way to ensure our library department gets enough money to keep our doors open?" represents a problem space far too complex to handle in one or two moves. In the real world of problem solving, the administrator is often faced with choices among many possible operators. Determining the best sequence of using the correct operators and moving the department toward the desired goal state often requires time, thought, and input from many sources. Oftentimes, a decision cannot readily be made and is pushed aside until it becomes too big to ignore any longer.

## Using Heuristics to Solve Problems

Heuristics or "rules of thumb" are experience-based techniques commonly used by public administrators and problem solvers in attempting to handle complex problems. Three common heuristics are "generate and test," "the hill-climbing strategy," and use of subproblems.

The most obvious way to attempt to solve a problem is simply to test mentally every possible path leading from your current state to your goal state. This imaginary process of trial and error gives consideration to all possible operators at every step. The "generate and test" heuristic can be random and time-consuming. It therefore isn't an extremely realistic or effective approach in helping us solve complex problems.

The hill-climbing strategy presupposes that the best path toward the goal state is always forward toward the goal. The maze-solving technique would be an excellent example of the hill-climbing strategy. In attempting to get out of the maze, we attempt to move in the direction of the exit. However, this strategy is fallible. The correct path often winds around, requiring you to take two steps back, away from the goal, before finding an appropriate route toward the goal. Public administrators sometimes have to unwind operations before moving forward toward their goal.

Another more effective problem-solving heuristic is to break complex problems into smaller subproblems. Experience tells us that people actually have greater success at problem solving using this technique. Our minds tend to work quickly when handling smaller tasks that have fewer operators and fewer paths to consider in solving them. In addition, in handling subproblems, we can more easily apply previous knowledge gleamed from successful handling of similar issues.

## Additional Problem-Solving Methods

Using one's common sense and attempting to apply rules of thumb to our problem-solving methods can be effective for easy problems or ones with which we are comfortable. However, with other problems we face, the methods can be a hit-or-miss situation. Sometimes they work, but more than likely they do not. Some general methods offer a better chance than others to help administrators gain at least a better understanding of the problem, if not solve it all together.

Some problems, especially those with which we have no familiarity, are best solved by starting at the goal state and working backward toward the current state. Many puzzle solvers will have success solving mazes this way. Working backward usually works well because there are fewer choices to consider at the end of the problem space than at the beginning. Therefore, using this strategy can reduce the overwhelming number of paths available at the initial state.

Reasoning by analogies or mental sets is one method that works for many public administrators. It is especially helpful when applied to several types of problems. With this method, problem solvers use their knowledge about previous problems that seem similar to the one at hand. One thinks, "I solved a similar problem this way, so I can probably apply the same problem-solving method to this problem and solve it, too." One looks for patterns in problems. When the same patterns appear, the theory is that the same problem-solving technique can be applied. However, using a mental set can also make it more difficult to solve a problem by giving one a false belief as to how something *should* be. The mental sets we choose to reason toward an answer to the problem often interfere with our ability to find the best solution because they create a belief that may not be correct. Individuals who have limited experience in problem solving should probably not rely on the reasoning by analogy or mental set option. Novices often tend to misunderstand patterns. They tend to apply superficial aspects to the problem space to make it fit a pattern that, in reality, does not exist.

One of the most useful problem-solving techniques, applicable in many problem spaces, is the use of imagery and diagrams. Drawing and applying mental images can clear away irrelevant detail from complicated problems and highlight important aspects that would otherwise get lost in the verbal description of the problem space. Many problem solvers find the use of imagery one of the best ways to define the problem space, particularly when the problem hinges on some spatial relationship issue. In many cases, it helps to draw a concrete picture of the problem rather than simply create a mental image. A physical image can be played with, reshaped, remodeled, and reinterpreted in a way the mental image may not allow. This can, in turn, produce new solutions to the problem that may not have appeared otherwise.

## Problem-Solving Traps

Regardless of the problem-solving method used, there are some potential land minds that problem solvers must avoid if they are to have success in reaching the goal state. Like mental sets and reasoning by analogy discussed earlier, using one's perceptions can also limit one's ability to understand the problem correctly. Perceptions cause us to apply our beliefs about the problem incorrectly and choose inappropriate operators based on those beliefs. For example, when we see "1/5 x 2/3 = 2/15," we may trap ourselves into believing that "1/5 + 2/3 = 3/8," leading us to an incorrect conclusion.

Another common problem-solving trap is called "functional fixedness." When administrators implore their staff to "think outside of the box," they are really telling them not to get trapped by functional fixedness. Functional fixedness causes us to impose unnecessary and sometimes unstated constraints. The problem of functional fixedness is normally the culprit when the problem solver is not able to recognize alternative functions of familiar objects. Instead, he or she fixates on the most frequent use of an object preventing the ability to think of alternative uses or explanations. The classic example often cited involves NASA spending millions and millions of dollars trying to design a pen for astronauts to use to write notes in space. The problem was that the ink in pens didn't always work upside down in space. Although NASA eventually did design a pen the astronauts could use, they were most likely a bit red-faced with embarrassment when the Russians, who were also looking for a solution to this problem, saved millions of dollars and hours of research by just giving their astronauts pencils! This example of functional fixedness showed how mental sets for various objects constrain us to think of that item in a single way and for one purpose, the way it was designed to be used. This often focuses our attention on that purpose, excluding others. The lesson for the problem solver is to rethink the object, look for other uses of the item, and let go of our perceptions.

## The Typical Problem-Solving Cycle

After having looked at a few of the basic and easier methods individuals typically utilize to solve problems, the reader may wonder how more difficult problems are addressed. There are formats that can be quite effective in tackling even the most difficult problems organizations may face. This section presents a fairly conventional problem-solving cycle and discusses the usefulness of employing a step-by-step approach to finding effective solutions to organizational problems.

1. **Agree that a problem exists.** It seems strange, but the initial stage in the problem-solving cycle is to identify that a problem actually exists. An organization should be in agreement as to whether there is a big enough gap between "what is" (our current state) and "what should be" (our goal state) and whether it is necessary to bridge that gap. Do people within the organization believe that "something is wrong and needs to be fixed"? Identifying the problem might be challenging for some. Perhaps the problem is encapsulated within a less obvious statement, such as "something threatens us and we need to prevent it," or "we're not providing something we should be." These sorts of gaps may have been identified in the SWOT analysis (see Chapter 6) during strategic planning sessions.

2. **Define the problem.** Once there is agreement that a problem exists, the next step in the cycle should be to define that problem well enough that we will know when we have solved it. Many administrators immediately jump into finding a solution to a perceived problem without knowing precisely what they are trying to solve. This leads to what is commonly known as "putting out fires" instead of fixing the problem. As an example, a library in which many staff members had complained that individuals were disturbing others by talking loudly on their cell phones responded by posting a big "no cell phones" sign. A few weeks later, there were more complaints from staff reporting that litter and spills were messing up the library's appearance. Management responded by posting a large "no food and drink" sign. Additional complaints from staff continued to come in regarding other issues, and management's reaction was to hang a sign saying "no this" or "no that." Posting signage may have dealt with some of the problem *symptoms,* but the true "problem" should

perhaps have been better identified. Perhaps the problem should have been identified as "why are the library's policies out of date with current user demands and practices?" Continually asking yourself, "Is this a *cause* of the problem or an *effect* of some bigger problem?" will allow you to understand the problem space better and ensure it has been correctly defined.

3.  **Problem analysis.** Once the problem has been defined, the process of looking for possible solutions can begin—the formation of a problem-solving strategy. Of course at this point, some of the heuristics discussed earlier in this chapter may have already been applied to the problem-solving cycle. For example, diagramming the problem, breaking a complex problem into manageable pieces, or working backward may have been early considerations of the analysis. However, information gathering, data collection, and research are essential to help us keep solutions grounded in factual analysis. Eventually, "who, what, when, where, and why" need to be addressed so that strategies can develop. Analysis of the problem includes asking many sets of questions: "What specific objectives need to be accomplished?" "What decision needs to be made?" "Can the problem be solved in steps?" "Is a partial solution better than none?" "Is this an organizational problem or a personnel problem?" "Is there a deadline to solving the problem?" "What resources are available?" "Is this a problem a group could solve?" "Who should be included in helping us solve the problem?" After answering these questions and analyzing the problem, you will have developed a frame around it. With the problem now contained within a framework, the cycle proceeds into the next step of generating some concrete solutions that fit within that frame.

4.  **Generating solutions.** When we think about problem solving, this is usually the cycle we envision. During this cycle, we develop a list of alternatives and possible solutions to the problem at hand. Perhaps we envision a group of people sitting around a huge conference table, one person standing at a flip chart writing down ideas as those around the table voice out, "We could do . . ." or "How about we . . . ." The more ideas gathered, the better. It is important to note, however, that solutions need to be contained within the framework developed in the earlier step. The framework was developed through a process of information gathering and research, and so connecting solutions to that data is important. The use of idea generating and decision-making techniques (which is discussed in the next section) will help give the administrator or problem solvers a good selection of choices from which to work.

5.  **Evaluating ideas and choosing a solution.** After collecting many ideas and giving these ideas a chance to settle ("sleeping on it," if possible, is certainly a good practice), a decision will need to be made about which of the ideas are most likely to solve the problem. The problem solver evaluates the ideas generated, considering the merits of each in solving the problem for the organization. Thinking of the pros and cons, the benefits and the detriments, of each of the possible solutions is critical. Do not fixate or focus on a single solution. Decide what the best three or four solutions may be. In choosing a solution, the problem solver evaluates which will offer the most effective (will work the best), efficient (costs the least resources—time, money, emotional baggage, etc.) path to the desired goal. At the same time, consider which will cause the fewest "side effects." Decision making tools are useful in helping choose the best solution.

6.  **Implementation of a solution.** At some point, action needs to be taken; a solution needs to be tested. Perhaps consider implementing the solution as a pilot project (trying it on a smaller scale before applying it throughout the organization). The key concept here is to put your solution to work as soon as possible. Sometimes administrators wait too long to implement a solution, trying to rethink their assumptions, reconsider data, and second-guess their assumptions. In our attempts to be cautious and take our time, we sometimes choose doing nothing rather than taking a risk. Not implementing a solution or abandoning a solution path too soon are common missteps in the problem-solving cycle. Solutions may take a while to alleviate a problem, so give it time to work.

7.  **Evaluating and follow-up.** Obviously administrators need to use their judgment and monitor the implementation process closely. Do modifications need to be made? Do other solutions need to be selected and tried? Is a different approach needed? Solutions may take some tweaking and adjusting, and remaining flexible to these changes is beneficial. The administrator's goal must always be to solve the problem rather than implement the solution exactly as it was proposed. Following up to ensure that the solution has actually solved the problem without causing any of its own is a final step in the problem-solving cycle. A common pitfall is that once a solution has been chosen and implemented, the organization assumes that the problem has been solved and people have wandered off or turned their attention away from the issue. Building an evaluation and feedback step into the problem-solving cycle will ensure that the solution you have chosen has worked effectively.

# Decision-Making Tools for Public Administrators

Up to this point in our discussion of problem solving, we have not addressed the notion of solving problems exclusively in the public service area. Certainly group problem solving, heuristics, and the use of the problem-solving cycle have application in making decisions and solving problems for public agencies. In public service, administrators continually seek to include many stakeholders (such as staff, council members, and the community) in the problem-solving and decision-making process. This ensures that a diversity of different opinions, skills, and talents are included and that there is a higher level of commitment to the problem solution once it has been selected. The remainder of this chapter discusses specifically the decision-making tools most often used in making decisions and solving problems for public agencies.

## Brainstorming

With the premise that one increases the odds of finding good ideas by first attempting to gather lots of them at one time, brainstorming has become common practice in public service when it comes to problem solving. Brainstorming is one of the most popular group problem-solving methods used. The method encourages spontaneity and creativity by asking the group to participate vocally in generating as many solutions to an identified problem as possible. It is explicitly stated that no judgment will be levied on any idea volunteered and that no idea should be thrown out. Normally a recorder or note taker writes down on a visible flip chart for all to see any suggestions that are called out. The ideas must be written out and visible to all because one idea may generate another idea, and someone can "piggy-back" off someone else's idea.

Brainstorming generally has three phases. First, there is the idea-generating phase just discussed. Second, the larger group breaks down into smaller ones, and some analysis of the ideas takes place between members of the smaller groups. During these discussions, group members seek clarification of ideas, discuss unfamiliar ideas, and define terms used. The groups then establish criteria for how to select the best ideas. They then evaluate each of the brainstormed ideas against those criteria, selecting what they feel is the best solution. Finally, once the groups have chosen solutions, the larger group reassembles as a whole to determine the steps necessary to implement them.

## Nominal Group Technique

"Brainstorming with a bit of a twist" best describes this decision-making process. Nominal group technique (NGT) starts with smaller groups brainstorming. Each group is given an open-ended problem statement. An open-ended problem statement is one in which there may be many appropriate solutions, and several appropriate paths to the solution. Open-ended problems encourage critical thinking because they are vague and may have many ways to interpret them. Some examples of open-ended questions or thoughts could be: "the best way to increase use of the library is . . ." or "the most important concerns in teen service facing our library are . . . ." To optimize the group's critical-thinking skills in the NGT, detailed clarification of the problem, such as providing specific examples to the group, is discouraged.

Unlike the brainstorming techniques, each member of the small group *silently* writes down as many solution ideas relating to the problem as they can. After a bit of time, group members share the ideas from their lists without any discussion or clarification. These ideas are all written out by a recorder for all to see. Within each group, discussion proceeds around the table with each person in turn sharing one idea from his or her list. No discussion other than clarification is permitted. The recorder writes the idea on newsprint for everyone in the group to see.

At this point in the NGT, discussion and clarification is encouraged, and group members are asked to agree or disagree with ideas and then choose four or five of the best ideas generated by the group. All the small groups are brought together, and the top four or five ideas from each group are joined together and written up. The entire group is then given instructions for picking the first, second, and third best ideas from all the ideas displayed. A useful technique is to give each member in the large group three colored adhesive dots. Each dot relates to a point system, that is, red dots are worth five, blue dots are worth three, and yellow dots are worth one. Participants then move around the room sticking dots next to the ideas representing their priorities. The votes are tallied, and the top solutions revealed.

## Charette Procedure

Another popular group idea-generating and decision-making tool in public administration is the Charette procedure. Its popularity stems from the fact that it addresses several aspects of the problem at the same time, allowing large groups to focus individual efforts on each issue in turn. The process involves small groups that each discuss parts of the larger problem simultaneously and then pass their ideas on to the next group. That group then refines, enhances, expands, and ultimately prioritizes the list generated by the previous group.

The Charette procedure is particularly useful when a group has already decided what its goal should be but is unsure of all the details involved in how to implement it. For example, suppose a community group has decided to build a new library branch.

The group's task is now to decide how to implement its goal. The group decides to address the following issues:

- "Where should the new branch be located?" "Where will the funds to build the new library come from?"

- "How big should the library be?" and

- "How do we get city council to accept the project?"

A small group is assigned to work on each issue. The small groups brainstorm to generate as many ideas as possible regarding the issue they are working on. A recorder for each group writes all ideas on a flip chart. After a bit of time has elapsed, perhaps 15 to 20 minutes, the discussion is stopped. Recorders then take their flip chart and move on to the next group. The next group reviews the items listed, refines it, and adds its own ideas. The rotation continues until each group has discussed each of the issues. The last small group in the rotation prioritizes items on the flip chart. The large group reconvenes and announces the set priorities.

## Paired Comparisons

In the public sector, especially in libraries, money is tight, making it difficult to add new programs or services without first eliminating some to compensate. When thinking of new services or new programs and comparing them against existing ones and trying to decide which is best, a group will brainstorm and come up with some priorities to use in choosing. Occasionally the group, especially in the public sector where many agendas and constituents need to be addressed, feels *all* priorities or options they have come up with are equally important. This makes it impossible to choose how to proceed. The paired comparison process can assist in the decision making at this point. The group first lists in one column all the existing programs it has chosen as "important" and in another column lists the several new programs under consideration. The group then starts with the first program listed in the first column and compares it against each one of the new services in the second column. With each pair of programs between Column 1 and Column 2, the group chooses the one priority. The group then moves to the second program listed in the first column and does the same until each of the programs in the first column has gone through a comparison with the programs in column two. By the end of the comparison, the program that has been chosen the greatest number of times is the priority service. The program or service that has received the fewest priority choices should be eliminated, if necessary.

## "I wonder if . . ." Charting

Many public administrators are faced with sensitive, often emotionally charged, decisions to make: "Should we allow food and drink in the library?" "Should we eliminate fines for children's books?" "Should we limit the number of DVDs a person can checkout?" and so forth. Brainstorming, although always helpful in generating ideas, can often shut down rapidly when one or two of the more vocal and powerful members of a group negatively influence the idea ("NO! That's a bad idea." or "We've tried that and it didn't work!"). A Pros/Cons chart acts as a brainstorming session but serves to bypass our naturally reactive and emotional judgments by exploring a controversial situation from the positive side first.

A group leader states the sensitive decision to be made and quickly leads the group through a brainstorming session, focused first on all the things that are good and positive about the issue. "What are the pros or the plusses if we do this?" The leader immediately calls for participants to name something positive, having these quickly written out on flip charts for the audience to see. The thinking must be done very quickly, perhaps no more than 4 or 5 minutes, so that negative thinking does not creep into the process. The leader may need to continually prod the group, "Come on, there has to be something positive?" "Good, what other thing do you like about this? Think like a user!" "One or two more pros, that's all, it should be easy." The enthusiasm of the leader in calling for positives first is important to diffuse the negative members from controlling the thought process. Next, the acknowledgment must come for the negative impacts of the decision, and the leader must give equal time to the group members to share those cons regarding the issue. Again, the leader quickly and forcefully leads the group toward its catharsis of negativity.

Once the pros and cons have been aired out, the group is asked to step back and consider all that has been written and to think of those things mentioned from another perspective. This time, the leader should ask the group to ask a question about the issue, starting with the phrase, "I wonder if . . .?" The leader may need to use examples from the list to start the process off. For instance, if the group was considering whether ambient music should be played in the library after school to calm students down, perhaps someone shouted out a positive that "I like to hear classical music in restaurants, and it would be nice to hear it in the library." Perhaps a negative was shouted out that adding music would only increase the amount of noise already in the library. Using these two comments, a good "I wonder if . . ." statement could be "I wonder if restaurants feel classical music helps their customers enjoy their dining experience?" Or "I wonder if certain music is more popular as ambient music in restaurants and why?" By focusing on these sorts of issues, the group can develop action items and do focused research that will help make a decision. Additionally, the group begins turning away from the emotional judgments and turns its energy toward exploring the problem from a reasonable perspective.

## Pareto Chart—The 80/20 Rule

A Pareto chart is a simple decision-making tool that is effective for separating the vital few from the trivial many. As a short bit of background, Vilfredo Pareto (for whom the Pareto chart is named) was a nineteenth-century Italian economist. He showed that 80 percent of Italy's wealth was controlled by only 20 percent of its citizens. Since his discovery, this ratio of 80/20 has been identified over and over in business and organizations, 20 percent of something produces 80 percent of the results. Even libraries have found that 80 percent of its entire circulation can be attributed to only 20 percent of the material in the library. When applied to problem solving and decision making, the 80/20 rule finds that only a few things, 20 percent of all the issues, account for the largest number (80 percent) of occurrences. The goal of a Pareto chart is to identify that 20 percent of something that accounts for 80 percent of the data results, and by addressing that small number, you will be solving the largest part of your problem.

The following example is presented to illustrate the Pareto chart in action. A library allows its users to request items from offsite, and it will hold them for pickup at any library location the user specifies. When the item is at the pickup location, the library user is notified that the item is now ready for the user to come and check out. The library system has found that many of the requested items library users have come in to retrieve are not where they are supposed to be, causing embarrassment for the staff and frustration for the customer. Analyzing the problem, a library group has generated ideas about why the problem occurs. They generate a large list of 25 ways the request process has broken down. This large laundry list of problem occurrences is impossible to tackle all at once. So the group decides to conduct a Pareto chart. The group lists all the problems on a sheet ("The item was incorrectly shelved on the hold pickup shelf," "The item was stolen off the hold shelf," "Another member of the family retrieved the hold," "The customer failed to pick up the item in the amount of time specified," and so on . . .). With all the possibilities for problems listed, data collection is completed throughout the library. For two weeks, each problem hold occurrence is logged, and the reason behind the problem is tallied. After the specified data collection period, all the data are tallied, and the Pareto chart is constructed. The Pareto chart points to three issues that are accounting for 80 percent of the problems. The library then manages to focus its problem-solving efforts on solving those three issues, and in so doing reduces its hold shelf mishaps by 80 percent. The 80/20 rule identified by Pareto has come in quite useful at this library.

# Choosing a Decision-Making Tool

The type of decision-making tool chosen will obviously depend a great deal on the type of decision to be made. Public administrators will need to consider the amount of time necessary for them to make the decision. An emergency situation requiring a quick decision will likely not be something to hand over to a large group or committee. Instead, emergency situations are often best dealt with by the leader of the organization or someone in top management. Another consideration would be the resources available in making the decision.

If the decision requires experts, special skills, or a substantial amount of money, the public administrator will want to consider assembling a larger group to include certain individuals with certain skills. The group could then use one or more of the decision-making skills discussed in this chapter. If a decision is already in the hands of a group, the decision-making tool chosen may need to address the history of the group's interactions and success or the climate the group wishes to establish. For decisions affecting a large portion of the community or the organization, the group may want to choose a tool that has the greatest level of participation in the process.

## Group Decision-Making Traps

For groups to make successful decisions, they need to use their resources well, choose the most effective tools, and receive high commitment to the decision from all members. However, even the most effective groups fall victim to common decision-making traps. The final section of this chapter identifies some of the decision-making traps common in public administration and provides tips on how to avoid them.

## Maintaining the Status Quo

"The way we have always done it" holds a great deal of power in the public sector. The public sector has a history of resistance to change. Change is uncomfortable for many, so the group gives bias to alternatives and means that perpetuate the status quo. In doing so, the group limits its ability to think of potentially better solutions and decisions. Alternatives that maintain the status quo do little to solve the problem. A group that has fallen into the trap of maintaining the status quo has stumbled at completing the first step of the problem-solving cycle: it has not identified that a problem exists. It has not seen that there is a gap between the current state and the desired goal state. The group needs to consider that, by making the decision to maintain the status quo, it has basically decided to do nothing. Is doing nothing the best choice?

## Confirming Evidence

Groups that have not successfully defined the problem will find it difficult to reach a decision. Without understanding the problem, group members begin to formulate "impressions" about the problem and instinctually come to conclusions. With these opinions in mind, group members will look for any data or information that confirms their initial point of view and avoid any information or data that contradicts it. Obviously this trap skews decision-making research by driving the group to certain people or certain areas of research to look for confirming evidence. It also leads us to interpret the data we get from others with a preconceived mind-set. Many public administrators fall victim to this trap by giving evidence biased by their past experiences and knowledge and look for groups or decisions that confirm them. To stay clear of this trap, administrators and groups should ensure that they are giving equal consideration to all evidence. Groups must ensure that they are not asking leading questions ("Doesn't the library need to continue interlibrary loan service?," "Isn't the front of the library beautiful?" "Don't you agree that these data are perfect?"). They should look for others in the organization to play the role of a devil's advocate and identify several negative issues about a decision.

## Anchoring

When people give disproportionate weight to the first piece of information they receive, they are falling into a decision-making trap, and this is known as "anchoring." Similar to the confirming evidence trap, anchoring a decision on the first thing you or the group sees or hears, without looking for other points of view, is a common fault in the decision-making process of many public administrators. Basing budget projections solely on what was done last year is a good example of anchoring. As another example, a new group member who forms impressions about the group's dynamics by talking to one of its members is falling into the anchoring trap. Groups and individuals making decisions need to be open-minded and resist forming early opinions without getting all the facts.

## Sunk Costs

In economics, sunk costs are those expenses made in the past that cannot be recovered. The tendency of groups and administrators to make a decision based on money that has already been spent is an example of the sunk-cost trap. Making choices that justify past choices, even when those choices are no longer valid, creates a situation in which we will likely prevent ourselves from making the best decision for our organization in favor of validating our previous decision. The classic example is supervisors who recognize that they have passed a bad employee off of their probationary period and now refuse to pursue terminating that person simply because of the amount of time, effort, and money already spent in training the individual.

## Framing

A decision should not be made on the basis of how well the information has been presented. The frame in which data are presented can skew the way we think about the information, causing us to react in a way the person who has framed the presentation would like. Framing information is a useful advertising tool because it influences consumers by compelling them to choose a product without thinking of the reasons why they did so. For example, have you ever wondered why an advertiser does not say, "Our product contains 5 percent fat." Instead, the advertiser says "Our product is 95-percent fat free." Now consider the case when a teacher tells a student, "You got a B on your paper, everyone else got a C" versus "You got a B on your paper, everyone else got an A." In each of these examples, the data that you got a grade of B did not change. However, the same data presented in two different "frames" tends to cause a different reaction. Opinion polls typically frame data in a particular way to cause a reaction. One recent story reported on a national news show that 9 percent of Muslims felt that the terrorist attack on the World Trade Center on 9/11 was a good thing. The difference in reporting the poll in that manner rather than saying that 91 percent of Muslims felt the terrorist attack was wrong is a striking example of the power of allowing our decisions to be influenced by the frame or presentation of the data. Instead, decision makers should gather all the facts and present all data at the same time. They should also consciously examine the frame in which the information is presented before making any final decisions.

## The Overcautious Trap

A group faced with making a tough decision may spin its wheels trying to confirm, reconfirm, and double-confirm its decisions. In the group members' hesitation to stand firm on the facts they have gathered and analyzed, they either slow the process down by doing nothing at all, or they make decisions to be "on the safe side." Those familiar with decision making in government will notice this trap quite frequently. Groups or administrators who do not want to risk the potential of upsetting the city council, the staff, or the community limit their chances of making a reasonable decision based on a skillful and intelligent decision-making process. The best advice is to stop worrying so much. If the decision has been intelligently selected, and if it is based on a rational and reasonable process, it should easily be able to withstand any scrutiny or second-guessing by those who don't currently have the understanding that the group does. Instead, the focus will be on how to educate others about the decisions that have been made and the benefits the decisions provide to the organization.

Problem solving can best be accomplished with a team approach. Because most public library directors are plagued by problems with facilities, the next chapter provides an opportunity for testing your problem solving skills.

# CHAPTER 12

## Facilities Management

Most of the problems handled at the public library could easily be classified under one topic, library facilities improvement. Not a day goes by at most public libraries that an administrator is not faced with a problem, complaint, or some other issue involving the library's physical space, "The toilet is clogged," "The lighting is bad," "It's too hot in here," "There isn't enough parking," or "The rugs need shampooing." The list goes on and on. Additionally, only personnel costs outrank our facilities as the largest part of our operating budget. It seems fitting, then, to follow our discussion of problem solving by turning our attention to the area where many of our problems erupt.

Of course, many of these issues are "reactionary problems"—that is, we don't do anything about them until something happens, and then we react. However, public administrators have a duty to take a more proactive look at our public buildings. In so doing, public library administrators can perhaps prevent many of the daily problems they face. This chapter focuses on managing public facilities, providing the reader with the basic process of how to prevent problems, who to contact when they happen, and how to handle them when they do.

# Who Owns Our Buildings?

Public facilities, such as libraries, parks, fire stations, and city halls, are owned by the whole community of individuals who pay taxes in that jurisdiction. Most public property is to be made accessible to all individuals. Because of this public nature, public buildings are also protected by city ordinances and state and federal laws that mandate appropriate use of the buildings by the public. These "use laws" often restrict certain activity such as drug use, loud disturbances, and theft of library material, and also outline hours of operation.

Some city libraries and their boards of trustees adopt behavior codes that further restrict use of the public facilities—for example, addressing food in the library or specifying that public library bathrooms cannot be used for bathing. These public facility use ordinances and codes have been useful in helping library administrators reconcile their profession's long tradition of offering open access while recognizing the need to keep our buildings safe, comfortable, and secure for all. One very famous case in library literature is *Kreimer vs. City of Morristown, New Jersey*.

When library staff asked Morristown police to evict a homeless man from the facility because his habits annoyed other library users, the man brought a lawsuit against the city. Because the library was a public building, his First Amendment rights were violated when he could not use the facility as he saw fit. Initial rulings agreed with the man, but the higher court eventually overturned that ruling, saying that for libraries and other public buildings, although open to the public, use of the facility was restricted to a "limited purpose," that is, patrons should be engaged in activities associated with the use of a public library while in the building.

Although the ruling of *Kreimer vs. Morristown* is valid only in the states of New Jersey and Pennsylvania, the judgment taught library administrators that our library facilities are public forums, and whenever the physical condition of our buildings and their environment somehow restrict access or use, we expose ourselves to potential litigation. A bathroom stall that is perpetually "out of order" or unavailable to a handicapped person, a sidewalk that is cracked and could cause someone to trip, a patron who has on so much perfume that it infringes on someone else's enjoyment of the building —all these can lead to the city and/or its library board being exposed to lawsuits.

# Public Works

Although the public has contributed funds to purchase the land and build the facility, the city government has domain over its property and uses tax money and city revenue to maintain it. Cities usually give the public works department the responsibility of working with city personnel to maintain city property. As the "caretaker" of the community's buildings, when lightbulbs need to be changed, toilets unclogged, or cooling systems fixed, the public works personnel are asked to provide that service. The Department of Public Works in most institutions has programs that place facilities within the city on three activity cycles: preventive maintenance, corrective maintenance, and trouble calls.

Preventive maintenance activity is meant to ensure that buildings are safe and secure, and by preventing potential damage and deterioration they can extend the facility's life. Also, by attending to building deficiencies before they become problems, the city saves money on making major repairs. Staff members within the public works department have usually identified those systems within the public library that need preventive maintenance (air filters, fire alarms, and fire extinguishers), and they likely monitor their own internal schedule for seeing to the necessary maintenance.

Corrective maintenance occurs when a component or part within some larger system needs to be replaced. For example, public works may note that a heating coil or air compressor within the heating and cooling system needs to be replaced to keep the system at optimum operational standard. This is a proactive approach to equipment care, and one that recognizes that parts within our facility systems do break down from wear. Corrective maintenance helps manage the workflow by early detection and planning for replacement or repair. Occasionally major maintenance can be identified as a part of the public works schedule. Perhaps a carpet needs to be replaced, a roof needs sealing, or, plumbing needs to be revamped. Although major building work is usually contracted out, these projects have a great impact on public service and should be scheduled so as to impede public service as little as possible.

Trouble calls are the point at which the library staff will likely become closely involved in facility maintenance matters. It would be terrific if all system and building problems could be eliminated through preventive or corrective maintenance, but building problems occur and equipment breaks down without warning, often needing immediate repair. When air-conditioning has failed, lights have gone out, or toilets have backed up, staff must respond immediately to ensure that the services provided in that building can continue. Libraries are public facilities that are routinely open outside of normal business hours. Our staff is expected to respond to trouble at any time, with or without public works staff. Many local governments have internal practices about how to request emergency repair service from the public works department. Other cities use "call-out" handymen. Regardless of the operations used in requesting service for trouble at a public library facility, it is often expensive, cumbersome, and labor intensive. A later section of this chapter provides a tip sheet of sorts that can be used by library staff and administrators, in conjunction with the maintenance that public works performs on facilities, that can make trouble calls easier to deal with when they occur.

## Service Contracts

Public works departments often work with outside service providers to provide maintenance of a routine nature or requiring a specialized skill. Cities will contract services such as janitorial, electrical, plumbing, elevator and fire-system testing, HVAC, and landscaping. In hiring the services of these contractors and evaluating their delivery, the public works staff members develop the specifications for facility project needs, and they conduct the appropriate bid process as specified by the finance department. The public works department also negotiates the service contracts and oversees the services provided to maintain quality control, as well as to resolve issues.

## Public Works Facility Crews and Library Administrators as Partners

With much of the work done within and on our library facilities being completed by another department or contracted out to a separate vendor, library administrators and staff must ensure an open dialogue between public works staff and library staff so that they can communicate specific facility needs and problems. One area often overlooked by public library administrators is including public works staff as part of the overall strategic planning process of the public library. Public works staff has specific and unique information that can be invaluable to public library administrators involved in strategic planning. They should be knowledgeable about product trends, quality, and innovation. They can offer critical information about customer satisfaction of certain products. Public works staff can offer advice that would be useful in identifying opportunities and threats facing the organization of which the public library administrator could be unfamiliar. Public works administrators can gain value from working with library staff by advocating certain equipment and facility improvements that will help its own crews offer improved technical quality and control facility-related problems. When considering the future of our buildings, then, public library administrators would do well to promote the inclusion of public works staff to ensure effective system design, quality product selection, and service delivery.

## The Environment and Public Buildings

As is so in many other areas, there is a large push in the public sector to be more aware of our environmental footprint, that measure of how much we demand from our natural resources in relation to our capacity to regenerate them. This is sometimes embedded in our call for "green buildings"—those that use little or have little impact on of the environment around us, while reusing resources and sustaining ourselves without negatively affecting the earth. While we all want to "save the world" by being as environmentally friendly as possible, cities are driven to consider green facilities because they can also save money and ensure that our investment does not harm our community.

Much of the push for green buildings comes from the U.S. Green Building Council. Many new public buildings now seek certification from this agency for Leadership in Energy and Environmental Design (LEED). The LEED rating system for new and existing buildings is a tool used to evaluate how environmentally friendly a building is. The more points the building receives, the better, and cities can be granted stipends and credit for meeting LEED standards. Additionally, states and cities are quickly adopting codes that regulate water and energy use in their buildings. The goal of green building is to optimize efficiencies of its facilities while saving on cost and upkeep.

Public administrators will quickly be required to accommodate the community's demand for energy and environmental friendliness. Professional library literature has begun to cover and research this growing trend in facility management. It would behoove administrators to research this topic area and to become familiar with current legislation regulating energy efficiency in public buildings in their community. For new building construction, renovations, and facility projects, the public library administrator will need to work with public works and other city staff to incorporate green building elements within the planning and design phase.

## Public Building Inspection

To assist in preventive and corrective maintenance, public works personnel and the library director work to schedule routine inspections. The following list should give library directors an idea of what to expect in terms of routine maintenance. To prevent surprises, it will also be beneficial to ask the public works department staff to alert you to the various maintenance schedules and inspection results of the following building areas:

- Alarm systems—Security alarms, audio monitoring alarms, theft detection alarms, fire/smoke detectors, boiler and plumbing alarms, and others should be checked at least once a quarter. Many vendors provide these services as part of their annual maintenance fee. However, occasionally inspections fall through the cracks or get delayed. Public administrators must be aware of "who does what" in terms of alarm systems so that if an inspection is not completed, service can be called. If the public works department is charged with tracking maintenance schedules, this should not absolve the library administrator from ensuring that public works has followed through on inspections of this type.

- Sprinkler systems—Typically the public works department will contract a specialist with skills in testing these systems twice per year. Pressure readings need to be checked regularly to ensure that valves, pipes, and hoses operate without obstruction. Many fire codes require that maintenance schedules for sprinkler systems are easily visible and completed regularly. Additionally, it is a good idea to have at least a working knowledge onsite of how to turn off sprinkler valves if they malfunction. At one branch library, staff members were confronted one weekend with a severely leaking sprinkler head that ran for thirty minutes over stacks of books while they tried to locate a shut-off valve and contact the city's "on-call" repair person.

- Fire extinguishers—Fire extinguishers are tested annually. This is often done by contract through the city for all fire extinguishers in public buildings. Because fire extinguishers are used more frequently than sprinkler systems, public works needs to ensure they are serviced properly and routinely. Like sprinklers, the city's fire codes will often require that the maintenance of your fire extinguishers be posted and available for inspection. It is also good advice to have public works staff arrange a live, hands-on demonstration of how to use fire extinguishers properly. This is particularly useful for new employees or employees who may be unfamiliar with extinguisher locations and operations.

- Emergency exits—Check emergency exits monthly to ensure that they are not obscured by such things as boxes or equipment. Check that push bars function properly and that door alarm batteries on the exit alarms are active. Check that exit lights as well as backup emergency lights function correctly.

- Floor and wall cracks/problems—Floor and wall cracks can be a sign of significant erosion or building problems. Additionally, cracks allow insects and dust to enter the building while allowing heating or air-conditioning to escape. Far worse is the potential for accidental bodily harm because cracks can be tripping hazards. Many floor and wall cracks can be repaired, and once noticed, they should be discussed immediately with the public works facility crew.

- Lighting—One of the most common complaints in public library buildings is poor lighting. A bulb out over your stacks can make it hard to find material on the shelves and prevent users from using your facility. Far more problematic, exterior lighting issues can be a significant safety issue. The public works staff should have a backup inventory of bulbs and ballasts on hand at your public library site to facilitate quick replacement when necessary. Dust should be cleaned from lighting fixtures at least once per year to maintain effective, sufficient lighting levels. Finally, staff should have access to a flashlight or mobile lighting implement to assist users in the stacks if bulbs cannot be replaced and this is causing problems with using your facility the way it was meant to be used.

- Heating ventilation and air-conditioning—The HVAC system maintenance will likely be completed annually. The scheduled service will check HVAC filters, fans, belts, and compressors to ensure they are running optimally. Routine and regular preventative maintenance will ensure that the system lasts longer without the need for costly repair.

The goal of any maintenance program the library director and public works department implement should be to identify the greatest risks to the library's ability to operate. If the library needed to be closed for four hours because of a system problem with the HVAC, what effect would that have on your community? Define the pieces of equipment or the places around your facility that will paralyze your operation if they fail. To prevent that from happening, you need to keep on top of the necessary preventative maintenance in these areas in particular. The public library director who shows a willingness to invest in maintenance and to work with the public works department in partnership to prevent building problems will have fewer complaints from their community. Additionally, resources will be spared, and frustration on the part of the staff will be reduced.

This chapter has outlined the challenges for making sure your facilities are safe for your patrons and has suggested that working with the public works office is always a good plan. In the next chapter, you will learn how to know your community.

# CHAPTER 13

## Knowing the Community

The root of so much that public library directors need to be successful lies in how well they know their community constituents. The strategic planning process cannot design appropriate services if the administrator does not know key wants, needs, and demands of the community. The library director and staff cannot communicate effectively with the community without knowing something about the people receiving that information. Managing and designing our facilities will be done far more effectively once we determine hard facts about who the users of the facility will be. To offer public library service effectively and efficiently, the director must start by constructing a frame much like the person constructing a puzzle builds a frame to make putting the puzzle pieces in place easier. For the public library director, this frame comes in the form of community analysis and needs assessments. Community analysis helps directors to summarize and characterize many of the common denominators within the community, including the people, their age, where they live, where they work, and other information. This chapter provides the reader with the steps involved in completing a basic analysis of the community.

## Community Analysis Goals

It should be noted that many library directors place such a great importance on completing a community analysis that they enlist the help of an outside consulting firm. These consulting firms, using sophisticated tools and technology, unleash large teams of survey takers, focus groups, committees, and task forces to gather as much community information as possible. Obviously this comes at a high price because consulting firms charge significant fees for the amount of energy, time, and other resources necessary to complete a thorough analysis and provide their client with useful data about the community. Why do library directors place so much stock in knowing about the community? A public library exists to make certain that the library's mission and purpose match the community's expectations and demands. Until a library can show its community that it is meeting user demands, it cannot truly consider itself successful. The process of completing a community analysis helps the public library director and staff articulate answers to specific questions about potential community demands. This, in turn, provides help in strategizing for the future; it helps the library staff design appropriate services; it helps collection developers select appropriate materials; it helps directors build appropriate facilities; and it helps the library staff to communicate effectively with its community, council, city staff, and library board.

Public libraries with the funding and time to contract with a consulting firm to complete a community analysis can certainly enjoy some pragmatic benefits, for example, an increased level of impartiality, complete focus on the project, and unique or specialized analysis skills. However, few libraries have the luxury of using those kinds of resources. Luckily, a consultant is not a necessity in completing a basic analysis of the community. In fact, many public library directors and their staff complete some element of a community analysis on a daily basis, such as looking at collection statistics, library use statistics, registration statistics, and program attendance. A more formal community analysis can—and should—be completed. Quite literally anyone can complete a good community analysis given the proper tools, attention, and commitment. The key to success is to keep in mind some basic community analysis goals. These goals should answer the following questions.

### Who Lives in My Community?

- Geographically, where are the majority of people in my community located?
- What are the people in my community most interested in?
- What do the people in my community expect from their library?
- How has my community changed over the past few decades?

- How is my community likely to change over the next few decades?

- What can I expect users in the future to want from their library?

There are many routes to answering questions such as these. Certainly some routes are better than others, and some methods seem to work better in certain towns and cities, whereas others contain steps and methods that do not make sense to apply to a small community. Still, by following the few basic steps that follow, the public library administrator will get a great head start in successfully describing and analyzing the library's community.

## 1. Defining Your Service Area

In beginning the community analysis process, the first consideration should be to define the geographic borders of your service area. Perhaps your governmental unit delineates the actual streets and residences that constitute the library's community borders. Perhaps you've used ZIP codes or geographic monuments to illustrate to your community that "this is the point where our library community begins and another jurisdiction's library provides service for those on the other side." However, issues such as these are never that easy for the public library director. Consider, for example, the complexities of a multibranch library system that serves an entire large city. Does each individual branch define its surrounding community as its only service area, with the central library considered a "branch"? If all citizens have equal access to each branch's service, perhaps it would be more appropriate to consider the entire city as the library's community.

A community could certainly be defined as just a group of citizens living in one particular geographic area. However, this does not allow flexibility for serving those "transient" citizens who live in one place, but who work, shop, and spend tax dollars in another area. In fact, many people might actually spend far more time and money in a community other than the one in which they actually live. How should the director account for these people when defining the community? They don't live in your geographic area, but they certainly use your service. Shouldn't the library's service area include these people? Most library administrators would say, "probably not," because if that were the case, the moment the Internet made it possible for anyone in the world to *virtually* locate and use your services via your library Web site, your service area could then be defined as the entire world!

### *Legal Service Areas*

It certainly seems impractical to think of the entire world as your service area, so many city, county, and state governments consider the "legal service area" instead. The legal service area is loosely defined as the borders that contain citizens to whom you are financially accountable, that is, local taxpayers. If you are accountable to the citizens of the entire city in which your library exists, then the safest bet is to define your library service area as that community made up of those who live within the city boundaries and pay for the library to exist through property taxes, fees, and sales taxes.

### ZIP Codes

When a service area is hard to define, many collection developers use ZIP codes. ZIP codes were created by the United States Postal Service to designate various postal delivery routes and residences. In some instances, a ZIP code might be far too broad to use in defining a library's local community. Nonetheless, most any retailer would tell you that roughly 80 percent of their store visitors, or in our case, our library visitors, come from within a radius of about one or two miles of the building's ZIP code. The farther a person is outside that radius, the less likely he or she is to visit the facility. A ZIP code, then, will help you identify that radius, allowing you to concentrate on that immediate neighborhood within your library's ZIP code area. This ensures that your services can be tailored to meet the needs of the largest portion of users and potential users. One final reason to use the library ZIP code as a starting point for defining the library's borders is the ease it offers in collecting critical data for the community analysis process.

## 2. Community and Neighborhood Immersion

Many public library directors drive to the library, spend eight hours within the building working, and then drive back home, never once physically visiting the neighborhood that the library shares. Public directors and all public library staff in fact can gain immense benefit from spending time within the community they serve by eating where the community eats, shopping where the community shops, and seeing what the community sees.

Not only will directors gain a better sense of the demographic and geographic complexities of the library service area, they will learn valuable lessons about community wants, needs, and demands. For example, if you visit the local grocery and department stores around the library service area, you could very well notice the magazines they are reading, the toys the children are buying, the foods they are eating, and the languages they are speaking. When designing library services, then, the director is better equipped to incorporate what they have learned and know about the community's trends.

During the community stroll, take along a community map to notate where schools are located, where the churches and shopping malls are in relation to the library, and other "gathering holes" community members gravitate toward. As people leave these areas, do they pass the library? How can the library connect these areas of the neighborhood with the library's services?

Looking around the community is certainly important, but don't neglect listening as well. Casually note discussion topics between parents at the local fast-food restaurant. What questions are people asking the clerks at the hardware store? What issues are the elderly concerned with at the local senior center? What are dads talking about among themselves at the soccer and baseball fields? Again, these observations may provide valuable clues to what the community expects from its local government and for which services and materials they are likely to expend time to visit the library.

## 3. Data Collection

Data comes in many forms. For all intents and purposes, the director will focus on just two, statistical and anecdotal. Readers are likely familiar with the difference between statistical data, which are factual in nature, and anecdotal data, which are based on what we *believe* to be true.

Statistical data encompass a majority of the data collection necessary to collect to ascertain intelligent information about your community. Some data such as demographics simply cannot be ignored. Luckily for the library director, statistics are fairly easy to obtain. Much of the necessary statistical data have already been collected by other departments or agencies. The U.S. Census figures describe age, income, sex, and education. The local school district counts the numbers of children in schools. The city's planning and finance departments each make an immense effort to perpetually collect statistical data useful to library directors completing a community analysis.

Because a community's needs and behaviors can vary significantly depending on its demographic character, public library directors should focus their statistics collection effort on learning as much about the current demographic makeup, its trends, and its anticipated projections. Some of the data topics public library directors should focus specifically on collecting include the following:

- Age—One of the most significant population dimensions of city public administrators, including the library administrator, is age because of its implications for service needs. Obviously children, teens, and adults have different needs and expectations.

- Ethnic diversity—A clear understanding of the racial and multiethnic composition of the community provides the director with unique data about the cultural expectations of users who are often neglected when designing city services. In city administration terms, the complexities of ethnic diversity often explain the economic, ethnic, and racial segregation within the city, often referred to as the divide between those who "have" and those who "have not." Layered upon the importance of understanding ethnic diversity is the implication it has on age, sex, and other demographic information.

- Educational attainment—Public administrators designing and adjusting services need to know the level of education and literacy members of its community have acquired. The level of education determines employment, which, in turn, determines discretionary income, living conditions, and, for the library public director, potential information needs and demands.

Anecdotal data come from the observations people make rather than scientific study. These observations are made, for example, by the director and staff as they immerse themselves in the neighborhood. Anecdotal data are based on feelings and judgment. For example, "I see a lot of Spanish billboards in my neighborhood; therefore, this community must have a very high percentage of Latino residents." For the public library director making new decisions about library services and justifying previous ones, statistical data carry a great deal more weight because it is harder to argue with the facts. Still, directors who ignore anecdotal data neglect an opportunity to enhance their knowledge and analysis of the factual evidence. Anecdotal data can be quite useful as a starting point for formulating a theory or hypothesis, which is later validated by hard statistical facts.

Most public libraries use some form of automated checkout system that can provide staff with copious amounts of statistical data regarding who is using your library services—in particular, your collections. Numbers of checkouts and numbers of new borrower registrations are often able to be filtered and drilled down into even more meaningful specific statistical data. For example, if your library card registration process collects birth-date information, you could easily track such numbers as "new male borrowers who are under age 26" or "use of fiction material by males versus females." Remember, however, that circulation-related data, although important, measure only current borrowers. They do not address nonusers in your community. In addition, circulation data provide evidence based on specific individual behaviors rather than controlled, clinical studies.

## 4. Making Sense of Your Data

Once the data has been collected, the director and library research team need to translate the data and make them mean something. The question they should continually ask is, "So what does all of this information mean to the library?" Remember the basic goals of the community analysis stated at the beginning of this chapter. How does this information help answer any of those critical questions?

It might be useful to start with easy, general concepts such as, "Our community analysis shows we have more women than men, more children under age fourteen than people over age forty-five, more homeowners than renters, more people with college degrees than without, and more people living in the south part of the city than the east. With these easy statements, the research group can begin to broaden its analysis by delving into the anecdotal data: "I assumed this was a conservative community, what statistical data support this assumption?" "My data tell me there are a large number of children in the community. What anecdotal data did I notice that enhance my understanding of that fact?" "I noticed that there were quite a few people renovating their homes. Could that imply that this is an older and more static community?"

Certain social indicators and demographics can be used to predict library use patterns and behaviors in your community. Community members' gender and education level, for instance, affect their demand for library service. Much of this information has been reported in library literature, and it bears noting here as well:

- The older people get, the less they use a library.

- Women use libraries more than men do.

- Up until the postgraduate level, the more education a person acquires, the more he or she makes use of the public library. Library use decreases, however, after the postgraduate level.

- Persons with a low income or a high income make very little use of the public library.

- Families with children are the heaviest users of the public library.

- The farther individuals reside from the public library, the less likely they are to use it.

## Projections and Estimates

When using demographic or other statistical data regarding your community, it is helpful to use the most current data. The U.S. Census data, which is one of the most popular sources of demographic community data, are only gathered and published every ten years. Once you are at the tail end of the census cycle, the previous data could already be well out of date. In a fast-changing community, using out-of-date information can be a critical mistake. Instead, directors should acquire estimates and projections about community data. However, you must recognize that these sets of numbers are hypothetical. As such, you must always use these numbers cautiously because estimates and projections *may* describe the probable and possible future, but there are no guarantees that they do.

An *estimate* measuring past and present conditions cannot be measured precisely because of lack of time or other resource. The U.S. Census uses sophisticated mathematical formulas in conjunction with information such as birth and death rates, voter registration, vehicle registrations, and other data to make an estimate of what to expect in many communities until the next round of data can be collected.

*Projections,* on the other hand, are less sophisticated assumptions of what is likely to be in the future if a given set of assumptions remains true. For example, if past growth shows a year-to-year growth increase of 3 percent, it is easy to project that next year's growth will equal that.

# Presenting Data

After collecting data and giving meaning to the numbers, the library administrator focuses on ways to present the data so that specific actions can be taken if necessary. Obviously, the community analysis was not done in a vacuum, nor would a library administrator consider expending time and money on performing an analysis if there was not some intended consequence. Perhaps the data were collected as part of the planning and SWOT process. Perhaps the data were collected to assist the library as it struggles to match service needs with budget cutbacks. Whatever the case, the way the data are presented can enhance its overall effect. Reviewing the information regarding budget presentations provided in Chapter 5 will benefit the reader, as it certainly applies to this topic as well.

After you have completed your community analysis, you can consider policies for your library. The next chapter explains the procedures for the development of policies.

# CHAPTER 14

## Public Policies

Young children will often play games without having any structure or parameters. They just make up rules as they go along. As children grow older, they recognize that guidelines are practical and bring structure and fairness to the game. Policies function as a type of "rules of the game." Everyone can play to their maximum potential if all players follow guidelines. Much of what public administrators accomplish relates directly or indirectly to public policy and policy decisions. In this chapter, we focus on policy dealing with how it is formulated and implemented. How do public policies affect city government? What is the importance of administrators in the policy process?

## What Is a Policy?

A policy is a statement that spells out the organization's philosophy, position, and operations. A policy is directed only toward those items within a department's jurisdictional control. They relate only to the foundation and principles to which the service extends. For example, it would be pointless for a library director to establish a policy dealing with its position on foreign wars. The library holds no jurisdictional control over if or when a foreign war can be declared. However, it does make sense for the library director to establish a collection development policy because such a policy affects the core purpose of the library's existence.

Policies help everyone understand why a service is necessary and provides the foundation for what the service accomplishes. A policy should be distinguished from operational rules and procedures. Unlike a hard and fast rule, the policy is more of a guideline or a principle. Policies don't say specifically "how" something is accomplished. A policy provides the overall framework, whereas a procedure presents a step-by-step approach to how a policy is implemented through a particular process.

## Public Policy Making

Local government officials such as city council members and boards and commissions within individual departments of public agencies are the ones charged with setting policy. The process of setting policy is done as part of the political process. This establishes an accountability link. The public can hold politicians accountable to the policies they create. If the public does not approve of the policies, then the public can deny that politician from holding future public office.

When it comes to creating public policy, policy makers face two unique outcomes. First, and perhaps the most ideal, is to envision as a team a desirable future condition and then to reach agreement as a team as to the best policies allowing the organization to reach its desirable condition. The other, and less desirable, outcome occurs when policy makers are unable to reach a consensus regarding a desirable future condition. In this later instance, policy makers blindly try to move away from their current situation, abandoning current policy without having any real consensus about where they would rather go.

Ideally, policy makers should be guided by core principles before creating public policy. For example, as public servants, we are accountable to the public. Special interests in public or private should not have the right to pursue their own interests without constraint. The decision-making process must be open and accessible; a sense of transparency should be the goal. Individuals and constituents within the community who are affected by projects and decisions must have the right to access all information regarding proposed developments; the right to challenge the need for, and the design of, projects; and the right to be involved in planning and decision-making processes.

# Library Board Policy Making

The primary function of the library board in most local government jurisdictions is to create and enforce the policies, rules, regulations, and bylaws necessary for the government, administration, and protection of the libraries under its management. That being said, most library boards look to the public library director for expertise in designing and bringing forward to the board any appropriate policies. As an example, consider the following case. At a library board meeting, several community members appeared before the board to make public comments regarding the use of the Internet computers at the library. Many of these community members were upset because the library was not providing enough access. With so few computers at the library, if individuals got on in the morning, they were allowed to stay on as long as they wanted. This caused a backlog of users. Some of the community members complained that while they waited to use the computer to type a resumé, others were playing games and chatting. The library board sought clarification from staff members as to how the Internet use was handled. As the discussion progressed, it was clear that the library's existing policy on computers was woefully outdated and needed to be addressed. Board members, who were legally not allowed to take action on the matter because it was not an item on that day's agenda, asked staff to bring back the policy for changes to a future meeting. The library board president further instructed the library director to work with the community members in creating a sample policy and appointed an ad hoc committee of two library board members to assist. In this case, the library board has the "power" to create a policy on its own accord. However, because they are not the experts, they chose to defer to the guidance and knowledge of the public library administrator.

Regardless of how policy suggestions come to the attention of the library board, all policy decisions remain their responsibility. The board should carefully review the policy, ask for changes if necessary, and approve the policy. The library director, then, will be expected to implement the policy and ensure that all library staff members are aware of it. The library board holds its public library director accountable for ensuring that staff members and library users follow the policy and know why it is in place.

# Policies Should Be Proactive Rather than Reactive

Creating a policy in the midst of a crisis or emergency is the worst possible way to formulate policy. Board members confronted by angry citizens are much less likely to consider all sides of the policy issue carefully and will instead want to "put out the fire" as quickly as possible. In so doing, they will likely create additional problems down the line. It is necessary to think of how policies impact every constituent. If a library policy is implemented in one way, what are the implications on other operations? Will the policy create the need to change or abandon other policies? Will implementing a policy create a workload on the staff? These are the issues that need to be carefully considered in the policy decision-making effort. Taking a proactive approach to policy formulation means that, almost immediately after the strategic planning takes place, policy decisions will be considered. Questions need to be asked that help to identify existing policy that impedes progress toward the planning goals. In addition, questions need to be asked that help to identify areas in which policy creation will enhance the library's effort in meeting stated goals. This proactive approach allows staff the appropriate amount of time to suggest appropriate policies for the library board to review.

# Types of Library Policies

The final section of this chapter discusses some of the most frequently needed, changed, amended, or adopted policies public library boards will consider. Although not a complete listing of every policy, it does represent policies that continually pop up in professional library literature as problematic or in need of better understanding. If they have not done so already, public library directors should most certainly expect to assist their library board in addressing the following policies.

## Material Selection

This area of policy encompasses so many philosophical and core values of our public library institutions that it would be quite surprising to think that a public library does not have an existing material selection policy. Far more likely is the possibility that the library's existing materials selection policy is many years (if not decades!) out of date and in need of a complete overhaul. The material selection policy, which is sometimes a part of a larger collection development policy, deals with the type of materials the library selects and does not select, the reasons behind the selection or exclusion of materials, the intended audiences of the material in the library, and much more.

Also contained within the material selection policy—and most likely the point at which the library board is confronted with the need for it—is the "reconsideration policy." Outlining the public's right to object to material in the library, the reconsideration policy often includes the American Library Association's "Freedom to Read" and "Library Bill of Rights" statements. Boards will often need to address the materials selection policy to determine whether to censure an item and remove it from the collection, outlining the community's right to object to material in the library and ask that the staff "reconsider" why something has been selected or excluded.

The materials selection policy will usually include two other sensitive policy areas. The library's "weeding" guidelines, which determine the professional process through which librarians decide which books are no longer necessary in the collection are frequently questioned by the public. Policies regarding the acceptance and disposal of material donations also have a high percentage of attention afforded to them. Both of these policies provide an important base for handling such questions as, "Why did the library get rid of my favorite book?" or "Why didn't the library return the book I donated to you once you determined you didn't want it?" The limits within which material is kept or discarded can be areas of confusion for the public, and many library board members may be leading the charge to investigate these areas of the material selection policy in particular.

## Circulation

Sometimes referred to as the library's material use policy, the community must know how and why borrowing privileges are available to the community. Additionally, the need for fines and fees are normally articulated here. The circulation policy needs to address whether children are offered public library cards. It should clarify who accepts responsibility for borrowing behaviors, lost material, and other borrowing issues. Another area, and again one in which the library board will normally be confronted, that is covered in the circulation policy is the philosophy of open access. Our profession's responsibility to provide all information to all users can be an area of intense scrutiny in smaller communities. Users need to understand why the library policy allows children to have access to and also borrow material from anywhere within the library, even a book from the young adult or adult collections.

## Programming

At least several times a year, an article appears in one of the popular professional library journals regarding a library board that is handling a community outrage over a program the library offers. Complaints range from "that program has no place in a library" to "kids should not be allowed to go to that performer's program at your library." Complaints about a program or a performer can cause picketing, anger, and unwanted media attention. The library board will often be asked to explain how programs are planned, how they are scheduled, and how they further the library's mission. The purpose of a programming policy is to define the parameters for programs offered by the library.

## Unattended Children

Many library board members and library staff have become increasingly concerned with the growing number of young children left unattended in public libraries. As a public building, our users need to understand that because libraries are places in which children gather, it may attract people whose interest in children is not entirely wholesome. Therefore, library boards often request that policies spell out the fact that the library staff is not responsible for the supervision of children. Unattended children policies serve to protect their well-being, maintain an enjoyable environment for adult users, and outline the proper use of the facility by children. Furthermore, the community needs to understand the hazards and consequences of leaving children unattended.

## Patron Behavior

Dealing with difficult patrons is one of the most uncomfortable situations library staff members face. Having a policy in place articulating what is acceptable behavior in the library helps the library director and staff members decide when it is appropriate to ask a member of the public to leave the premises. Many libraries have adopted "codes of behavior" restricting certain unwanted behavior, and these codes bear the weight of potential fines and fees behind them should patrons choose to ignore policies. Some of the behaviors such as skateboarding, running, or bringing bikes into the library are meant to protect patrons from activities that could cause accidents and injuries. Other behaviors such as yelling, swearing, or causing a disturbance, are harder to enforce because they require library staff members to make a judgment call as to whether the behavior crosses the line. Still, the desire for library board members and administrators is to cull a policy that creates a library environment in which all library users and staff enjoy a safe, pleasurable, and nonthreatening experience.

Administrators should resist the knee-jerk reaction of some library board members to recreate the library of the past in which librarians were constantly "shhhhhhushing" people, and library patrons were expected to maintain a silent sanctum. Public libraries have evolved, and so, too, have the information-seeking needs and behaviors of our community members. The need for teens to study in teams and take advantage of social networking should be encouraged rather than discouraged because a library board member remembers "the old days." Additionally, administrators must insist that all users are served equally, including those who see a library as a place for quiet research and those who see the library as a community gathering place for entertainment. Public library directors should resist the pattern of suggesting policies that restrict or limit library use simply because one or two people abuse the privileges the library offers. As an example, the current "hot topic" in many public libraries is restricting cell phone use. Because several patrons disturb those around them by talking loudly on their cell phones, oblivious to their surroundings, should the library's board be encouraged to have a "no cell phone" policy? Absolutely not! Would the same library implement a policy that said "no texting on your cell phone"? Cell phones are a normal part of our everyday society. Most everybody has one, and the library board should not penalize 80 percent of the people who make perfectly fine use of cell phones because of the 20 percent who use them inappropriately. Instead, library users who use their cell phones inappropriately should be handled as a disturbing patron, and asked one-on-one to use their phones in a more appropriate manner so as not to disturb others. If the library user ignores the request, he or she can then be asked to leave, citing the patron behavior code.

The final chapter helps the library director carry out organizational change. This may be the most difficult area to implement.

# CHAPTER 15

# Implementing Organizational Change

Public agencies are not noted for their flair in adapting to changes even in their business world; quite the opposite, really. They are usually slow to adopt organizational change. Organizational culture within the public sector has, until recently, valued a sense of stability. The notion of the "status quo" with standard operating procedures, unchanging organizational structure, decision making from the top down, and inflexible policies have contributed to the notion that public organizations like public libraries are bureaucratic statues. For example, many public libraries refused to get rid of card catalogs in favor of online public access catalogs (OPACs) even after OPACs were in the facility! Our professional history is filled with such examples. We took years to provide DVDs; we didn't think it would be necessary to provide this thing called "the Internet"; and we resisted subscribing to e-books.

Professional literature meant for public administrators in recent decades, however, has been filled with articles emphasizing the need to develop our agencies and strive for innovation and change. This final chapter discusses the management of change. How do administrators plan for change? How do we implement it? And, finally, how is change communicated?

## Organizational Change in the Public Sector

The push for organizational change in local government and public agencies took root in the early 1990s when President Clinton's administration created the National Partnership for Reinventing Government. Spearheaded by Vice President Al Gore, the "reinventing government" charge was made directing federal agencies to reform the way they did business, to change the structure and approaches to how public workers performed their tasks, and to look for efficiency and effectiveness in serving communities. Most of what occurred was policy updates. Later in the process, government agency restructures improved the way citizens interacted with the federal government. Local governments, inspired by some of the success, began to look at their own operations. Elected officials placed expectations on city managers and public administrators to reinvent their own operations. Organizational structure, policies, personnel, and customer service seemed to be key areas of change, and public administrators embarked on changing management processes to tackle those very topics.

## Tips for Starting and Managing Change

Public administrators will soon be called upon to implement change processes within their own departments. Within the public library field, change management is perhaps one of the most common "skills and abilities" listed on library directors' job specifications and recruitments. Successfully leading staff through a difficult process of change is a critical aspect of administration. For example, at the conclusion of a strategic planning process, a director will likely be faced with a long list of goals and objectives meant to propel the organization from one level to a whole new level, perhaps adopting new service models or a new mission. And much like the process of team building, in which specific phases of progress were noted, there are definite phases through which the change process should move to increase its chance of success.

### Phase One: The Need to Change

Change should not occur for the mere sake of changing. For the change to occur, the organization's staff has to see the need. Creating a sense of urgency and need, then, should be the first step in the change management process. The library director must convince each stakeholder within the organization from the library board to the city manager to the custodial worker(s) that the current state of the organization is not desirable and that the organization needs to transform itself or risk all-out failure.

Communicating the forces behind the need to change, the consequences of inaction, and how things will be better after the change are imperative pieces within this implementation phase.

Directors need to recognize that their job is not to make people feel "happy" about the change. Their job is to make people feel comfortable with the need to change. Public library directors need to understand that those within the organization will feel awkward, ill-at-ease, and self-conscious. Staff and stakeholders will immediately begin to think of their comfort zone and the things that they have to give up. Instead of fearing what will be, they grasp on to the loss of what was. The strategy during this phase is simply to communicate to staff and stakeholders to expect these feelings. People will need to realize that these feelings are normal. It's important to legitimize the losses of "the way things were" and allow staff members to mourn. However, this should be immediately followed up with a reminder of the urgency to change and the benefits of the change.

## Phase Two: Building a "Change Team"

Public library directors who attempt to implement change by themselves are doomed to fail. Because the catalyst to change is so difficult to achieve, it requires a coalition of "movers and shakers" within the organization. A powerful force of "change cheerleaders," specifically selected for their leadership skills, their ability to instill trust and respect, and their expertise, will provide that needed spark to create and sustain the change momentum. When faced with significant change, people often feel alone even if the whole organization is going through the change. The team should look for ways to involve these staff members in the change process. Having a guiding coalition of change agents will encourage these staff members to share ideas and work together to make the change beneficial to everyone.

## Phase Three: Communicate, Communicate, Communicate

A fine line is drawn between a vision and a hallucination. The organization must believe that attaining the goal is possible. The public library director must continually seek to focus energy and attention on the goal state. The organization needs to be reminded of the difference between the current state and the goal state. To move an organization toward the goal, then, the goal must be continually made a part of the conversation. Communication is the most effective way to assure your staff and your organization's stakeholders that your vision is real. Readers are encouraged to review the art of communication discussed in Chapter 8 and make use of the suggestions for effective communication found there. Directors need to be reminded that lack of communication is often cited as the number one reason change fails. Combating that with successful communication at all levels is imperative.

## Recognizing Success

Public library directors often state that "declaring victory" too soon often sinks an otherwise successful change process. They are encouraged to give the change process enough time to become a part of the organization's culture before declaring they have reached their goal. A successful change implementation process can take several years or longer to fully instill itself into the organization. By taking the urgency out of the equation or by declaring that the goal has been reached too soon, people may revert back to old behavior. New policies may be fragile or imperfect, and some "tweaking" may not be immediately evident. The director must keep the change momentum going, preventing the tendency for old processes and traditions to crop up again.

Leaders of successful change implementation efforts use the feeling of victory as the motivation to delve more deeply into their organization. They foster a desire for the organization to embrace principles of continuous improvement and look for organizational systems that need tuning. Public library directors should be motivating their organizations and empowering their staff with new ways to achieve goals that help the organization reach new ones.

# Conclusion

The task of imparting to the reader "everything" there is to know about how to manage and administer a public library in the span of fifteen chapters is, in hindsight, a challenge more difficult than it seems. It is my hope that some of the basic elements involved in helping the reader understand the means through which public library administrators, especially those in small public libraries, create successful and relevant library services have piqued your interest enough to continue to study the art of public administration.

Obviously, however, this text will have prompted the reader to ponder additional questions, issues, or challenges that public library directors will come across in the course of their days. Many resources are now available on the Internet, in your local library, and at your local university which will lead the interested public library director further down the road to "expertise." However, the best way to learn is to watch and listen.

Find a public library director whom you admire and study them. What makes them successful? What decisions have they made, and why did they make those decisions? What process did they use to make the decision? How did they involve the community, the staff, and the library board in the decision-making and problem-solving process?

By learning the answers to these questions, you will immediately begin to understand how public administrators seek to improve services to our communities. Furthermore, by talking to colleagues, reading library professional literature, attending council meetings, and taking an active role in local government, the student will enhance the lessons learned within this book and become more and more comfortable with the heavy responsibility public library directors have accepted.

Public library administration is not brain surgery. Regardless of what anyone may tell you, interested persons can learn how to manage a public library effectively. By learning to be patient, flexible, and adaptable to change; learning how to work with shrinking budgets; being resilient; and following the basic principles outlined in this text, you, too, will soon find yourself at the top of the organizational chart.

# Index

# About the Author

WAYNE DISHER is public library director for the city of Hemet, CA. He is also a part-time faculty member with the San Jose State University School of Library and Information Science program in San Jose, CA. His published works include Library Unlimited's *Crash Course in Collection Development*.